CHAKRA FOR BEGINNERS

Awaken Your Spiritual Power
For The Healing Of The Mind, Soul and Body

EMILY C. HEAVEN

Copyright © 2020 – Emily C. Heaven

All Rights Reserved

Table of Contents

An Introduction to Chakras 5

History of Chakras.. 9

The 7 Chakras 11

and Where to Locate Them 11

   1. The Root Chakra (Muladhara) 12

   2. The Sacral Chakra (Svadhishthana) 14

   3. The Solar Plexus Chakra (Manipura) 17

   4. The Heart Chakra (Anahata) 20

   5. The Throat Chakra (Vishuddha)....................................... 23

   6. The Third Eye Chakra (Ajna) 26

   7. The Crown Chakra (Sahasrara) 28

Ways to Clean and Heal your Chakras 32

   1. Affirmations... 45

   2. Massages for balancing 46

   3. Color Vibration 47

   4. Chakra Stones 49

   5. Yoga for Chakra Healing 49

   6. Music for Chakra Healing 50

   7. Professional Energy Healers 50

   8. Essential Oils for Chakra Healing 51

How to Unblock Chakras? 55

How to Practice the Chakra Balancing and Activating Meditation?.. 111

Conclusion 113

An Introduction to Chakras

Everything in this universe radiates energy, from the biggest oceans or mountains to the tiniest cell in our body. Each cell in our body emits energy in different ways, depending on where it is located within the body and what job they perform. Chakras are the different channels positioned on key points of our body through which energy flows in and out in a constant stream.

Chakra is a Sanskrit word, which means "Wheel." Chakra energy spins in a counter-clockwise direction to pull energy from the outer world into the body, and it spins clockwise while moving energy from our body to the external world. There are seven chakras which exist at different points in our body: The Root Chakra (Muladhara), The Sacral Chakra (Svadhishthana), The Solar Plexus Chakra (Manipura), The Heart Chakra (Anahata), The Throat Chakra (Vishuddha), The Third Eye Chakra (Ajna) and The Crown Chakra (Sahasrara). Each one of these chakras is associated with a particular organ and system. Moreover, there are different colors associated with each chakra. The major question here is, how does a chakra actually work? A chakra may be a vortex or a wheel; however, it operates as an energy ball. It is not possible to see the chakras on an x-ray because they are not physical rather are aspects of consciousness. Chakras interact with the energetic and physical body through the nervous system and the endocrine system. The chakras are associated with the endocrine glands in the body. They are also associated with plexus (a particular group of nerves). Thus, it can be said that each one of these chakras corresponds with specific parts of the body and perform specific functions that are controlled by an endocrine gland or the plexus. This is the key to understand how chakra healing methods work.

In addition to representing physical parts of the body, chakras also represent parts of our consciousness. All our possible states of awareness, perceptions, and senses can be categorized into seven different categories, which can be associated with any one of these chakras. For example, if a person feels stress in his consciousness, he will feel it in the chakra that is associated with that particular part of his consciousness experiencing the tension or stress. Likewise, when a person is hurt in a relationship, he will feel it in his heart. When a person is nervous, his legs tremble, and his bladder becomes weak. Whenever there is stress or tension in a specific part of our consciousness or the chakra associated with it, the nerves of the plexus detect the tension, after which it is communicated to different parts of your physical and energy body. When this stress or tension continues for a longer time, certain physical symptoms are produced, thus requiring the chakra healing to resolve. The physical symptom leads to an imbalance in the energy of your body. Therefore, there is a great need to reverse it. It can be reversed via physical change and chakra healing practices. This tension can also be released by changing your ways of being. In this way, you will be able to return to your natural state of health and balance.

Another concept that is important to understand is the opening and closing of the chakras, which works just like an energetic defense system. A negative experience is associated with low-frequency energy. Whenever we have a negative experience, the chakra associated with it is blocked for the purpose of blocking that energy out. Likewise, when a person clings to a low calibrating feeling such as blame, the chakra is closed off. The reason is that it is the channel through which energy can escape. When the chakras are blocked, there is a need to heal or unblock them. Different chakra healing techniques such as the Fire Breath exercise can be used to heal the chakra. Once you open and heal your chakras, energy flows freely, and things return to normal in your body.

Chakra healing is very crucial. Each chakra is connected to the nervous system and an endocrine gland in your body. So, if you ignore the energy deficiency for a long time, it can lead to severe physical consequences. The most important key in chakra healing is "balance." It cannot be said that one particular chakra is important than the other. All the seven chakras in your body are important as far as the chakra healing and balancing is concerned. For example, a person cannot have low extra throat chakra energy and less heart chakra energy. It is not at all like that. All of the seven chakras in your body must be balanced, open, healed, and humming. Only then will they be able to transfer energy into your body or out of your body to the external world. One of the most important features of your body is that even if one of your chakras is underactive or closed, any other chakra may be overactive or open to manage the difference. If anyone of our chakras is overactive or underactive, it can have very negative impacts on the body. Therefore, our body always tries to maintain an energetic balance in all our chakras. The energetic imbalance can be counterproductive in the chakra healing process. When one chakra gets knocked out of balance, it can lead to an imbalance in any other chakra that may pull extra energy away from that particular part of the body. Thus, there is a need for balancing and healing.

History of Chakras

To properly understand the chakras, it is important to know their origin. The chakra system originated between 1500 and 500 BC in India (In the oldest text referred to as Vedas). The evidence of the chakras, originally spelled as chakras, are also found in the Cudamini Upanishad, Shri Jabala Darshana Upanishad, the Shandilya Upanishad, and the Yoga-Shikka Upanishad. A famous scholar named Anodea Judith mentioned in her book 'The Wheels of Life,' *"knowledge of the chakra system was passed down through an oral tradition by the Indo-European people, also called the Aryan people. The Chakra system was traditionally an Eastern philosophy until New Age authors, like Anodea Judith, resonated with the idea and wrote about the chakras, expanding upon the older texts and making the knowledge more accessible."*

A chakra is a wheel or spinning disk that runs along the spine of the human body. The health of each of your chakras is connected directly to your mind, physical body, and emotional well-being. Ever since the beginning, yoga and the chakra system have been intertwined. There are certain real truths about the chakras which everyone should know:

1. In the original tradition, there are many chakra systems, not just one.
2. The chakra systems are not descriptive rather prescriptive.
3. The psychological states that are associated with these chakras are totally modern and western.
4. The seven-chakra system that is popular in today's world derives from a treatise that was written in the year 1577, not from any scripture.
5. The major goal of the chakra system is to work as a template for Nyasa, which refers to the installation of deity-energies and mantras at particular points of the subtle body.
6. The seed-mantras go with the elements that are installed in the chakras.

The Kundalini and chakra system arose in the Tantric tradition during the Common Era. The major text about the chakras is a translation by an Englishman named Arthur Avalon in one of his books, "The Serpent Power," which was published in the year 1919. Various texts such as the Padaka-Pancake written by an Indian pundit in the tenth century and the Sat-Cakra-Nirupama written in 1577 contain portrayals of the centers and correlated practices.

The 7 Chakras and Where to Locate Them

With the help of simple exercises, you can easily locate the chakras, assess them, and potentially rebalance or realign them. Remember that all the chakras are associated with a specific element.

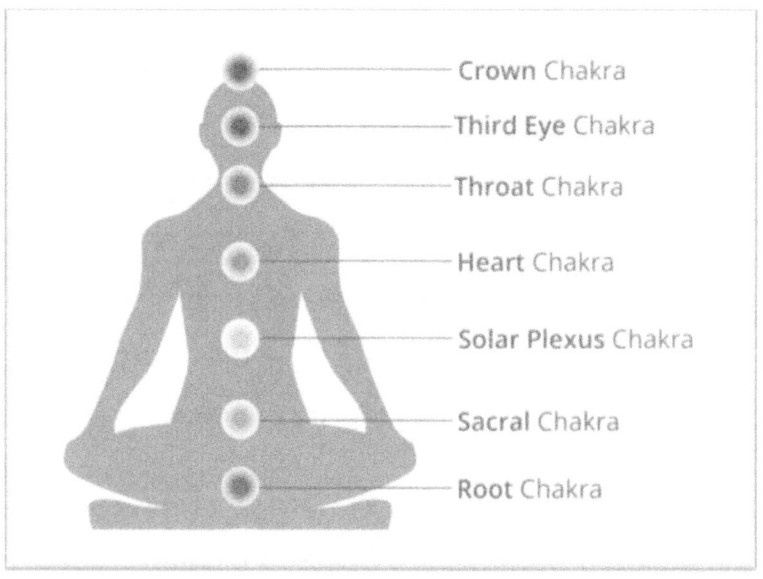

1. The Root Chakra (Muladhara)

The root chakra is located at the bottom of our spine, where the tailbone is located. The color associated with this chakra is red. This chakra is foundational. When everything is well with the Root Chakra, you will feel anchored, calm, and secure in reality. You will be able to handle difficulties and tackle challenges boldly. While doing so, you will feel very confident. The Root Chakra is very important whenever you try something new in life or when you pursue the major goals in your life. Whenever you feel that something is threatening your basic survival needs such as money, shelter, or food, you can unblock or heal your blocked root chakra. This chakra will respond even when you just have the fear that your basic survival is undermined. There are certain behaviors and emotional issues linked to a blocked Root Chakra. When the Root Chakra is blocked, a person feels anxious, panicked, and threatened. This anxiety can infiltrate our thoughts, which leads to feelings of uncertainty. When this chakra is blocked, a person might not be able to focus or concentrate well. He will lose his concentration over everything. Also, a blocked root chakra also makes a person feel that he is preoccupied with worries about his well-being. This can manifest as general paranoia or hypochondria in some people.

Moreover, a blocked root chakra also causes certain physical issues such as low energy levels, cold extremities, and sore lower back. Thus, it is important to balance and unblock your root chakra. To sum up, the root chakra is located at the base of our spine, and it deals with our basic survival needs such as food, shelter, etc.

Muladhara is a Sanskrit word, which literally means "base support." The root chakra is connected to your legs. Therefore it is a symbol of earth as well as all the other things that are solid and stable. This is the reason that the root chakra is the chakra of all the hard parts of your body, such as bones, teeth, and nails. The root chakra controls different parts of your body, such as the lymphatic system, sense of smell, bone system, nose, prostate, and lower extremities. This chakra symbolizes self-confidence, security, and stability. It is fundamentally related to your survival. When your first chakra or root chakra is balanced, you feel happy and safe. You stay enthusiastic all the time, and you can live or enjoy the present moment. Also, when this chakra is balanced, you can actively plan for your future and pursue your goals. When this chakra is blocked, you feel lost, distrustful, and lose your self-confidence. In case it is blocked, the person never feels satisfied in one particular place; he keeps changing house or country often.

Moreover, a person feels exhausted and tired. He might have problems with his kidneys, teeth, and joints. If you can rebalance your root chakra, you will start feeling happy. There are different ways through which you can unlock your root chakras, such as exercises, visualizations, and positions. Remember that to balance your root chakra; you do not have to fake pretending that you are happy. You will simply be able to heal following certain tips and measures.

Summary Sheet of the Root Chakra

- Position: At the base of the spine
- Color: red
- Function: Survival, security, stability, self-confidence
- Element: earth
- Sense: smell
- Mantra: Lam, S
- Stone: red coral, red jasper, ruby, garnet, oxidant, black onyx,
- Note: do
- Lotus: 4 petals with earth inside
- Animal: ox, elephant, bull (associated with the earth)

2. The Sacral Chakra (Svadhishthana)

It is the second major chakra in our body. It is also referred to as the second or the sexual chakra. This chakra is located above the genitals in the public area, just about 3 inches below your navel. It is called sexual chakra because it plays a key role in the regulation of sexuality, sexual energy, intimacy, and sensuality. The sacral chakra is the creative physical center. This chakra controls the urinary tract, pelvic organs, the hips, the bladder, feet, and legs. It also energizes the sexual organs.

The sacral or sexual chakra is polarized negatively, and it is feminine in gender. The color associated with this chakra is orange. If the second chakra is open and clear, you experience feelings of very deep feelings of childlike wonder. The world looks more like a magical place when this chakra is open. However, after puberty, a person experiences blockages in the sacral chakra because of the restrictions and taboos of the society related to sexuality. Because of this blockage, all the wonder and innocence are lost after puberty. This chakra is the focus of your most fundamental and earliest emotions, such as your basic sense of acceptance or rejection, the sense of being alone in this world, or belonging to a particular family or group, and the difficulty or ease of an individual may have in connecting with God. A person's sacral or sexual chakra may be blocked or misaligned when he is stressed or worried about any of the aspects of his sexuality. This chakra will also be blocked if a person is not satisfied in his relationship or is simply trying to experience pleasure in his life. The sacral chakra may also be blocked if you receive any sort of negative feedback, which makes your doubt your capabilities.

The blockage in the sacral chakra results in many emotional issues and behaviors. When there is any problem with this chakra, a person feels listless, uninspired, and bored. He will have a very low sex drive, and he might feel afraid of change. Also, certain physical symptoms are associated with a blocked sexual or sacral chakra. Some of these symptoms include increased allergies, attraction to addictive behavior, and urinary discomfort. Issues with eating, gambling, and shopping addiction can also be associated with a blocked sacral chakra. Other effects of the sacral chakra malfunction are contempt for sex, fear of pleasure, sexual repression, and energy blockages. All these limit the expression of an individual's personality. Keeping in view all these issues linked to the blockage in the sacral chakra, we need to heal and balance it. To heal or rebalance this chakra, a person needs to work on his emotions and creativity. Moreover, a person also needs to dedicate himself to certain exercises such as long baths, showers, swimming, etc.

Summary sheet of the Sacral Chakra

- Position: lower abdomen
- Color: orange
- Function: emotions, desire and procreation, sexuality, creativity
- Element: water
- Sense: touch and taste
- Stones: amber, opal, citrine, topaz
- Lotus: 6 petals with a half-moon inside
- Mantra: Vam, M
- Note: re
- Animal: crocodile, fish, snake, reptiles

To sum up, the sacral chakra governs a person's sexual needs. An open and balanced sexual chakra will lead to the smooth flow of sexual energy in your body. He will feel comfortable and will also be passionate about his relationship. An open sacral chakra ensures that a person does not have any sexual dysfunction. If a person's sacral chakra is underactive, he will lose interest and will be devoid of emotions. On the other hand, if this chakra is overactive, a person will be sensitive and emotional all the time. He might feel a constant need for sexual activity.

3. The Solar Plexus Chakra (Manipura)

Sometimes, this chakra is also referred to as the "Personal power" chakra. It is vital for autonomy, self-esteem, and determination. This is the reason that it is also called personal power chakra. When this chakra is open and balanced, a person will have a clear path ahead of him. He will feel independent and will be confident enough to accomplish great things in his life. The solar plexus chakra is located around your stomach area at the top of the abdomen. The color associated with this chakra is yellow, and the element linked to it is fire. If there is a blockage in this chakra, you will experience many emotional issues and behaviors. You will lose your confidence, and it will be very shaky. However, if the blockage is small, there will be insecurity in any specific area. A larger blockage will cause many self-esteem problems. A person may be haunted by thoughts that he is not good enough. Also, he might feel that he is not able to draw useful challenges from the challenges in his life. Certain physical difficulties are associated with a blocked solar plexus chakra, such as trouble with memory, digestive discomfort, etc.

The solar plexus chakra involves many parts of the body such as the stomach, skin, liver, muscle system, glands, large intestine, and other organs around the solar plexus, which is part of your abdomen between the navel and diaphragm. This chakra is also associated with the muscles of your face, the eyes, and the sight. It is connected to energy, light, and heat, and when this chakra is balanced, you will feel strong, self-confident, energetic, and self-controlling. This chakra is also connected to digestion and the digestive system. When this chakra is unbalanced, you will see many symptoms mentally as well as physically, particularly symptoms related to safety and the digestive system. When it is underactive, you will notice low self-esteem, the rise of insecurity, introversion, a very strong sense of inadequacy in different situations. As far as the physical symptoms are concerned, you will experience liver disorders, ulcers, nausea, gastritis, and coeliac diseases. This chakra is polarized positively and is masculine in gender. It has front and back entry points which are located opposite to each other.

Summary Sheet of Solar Plexus Chakra

- Position: solar plexus
- Color: yellow

- Function: self-esteem, power, strength, life awareness, expansiveness, will act, and pleasure
- Element: fire
- Stones: all yellow stones, in particular Citrine Quartz, Calcite, and Topaz
- Sense: Sight and Smell
- Mantra: Ram, U
- Note: mi
- Lotus: 10 petals with a ram inside
- Animal: ram, a symbol of fire

In conclusion, a balanced solar plexus chakra controls the liver, pancreas, diaphragm, gall bladder, appendix, small intestine, large intestine, stomach, appendix, blood, lymph, etc. This chakra is also responsible for the assimilation of food. Also, it plays a key part in an individual's relationship to people, places, and to the whole world as well as his ability to have a sense of belonging and feeling connected to the people around and the love of home, family, and country. When balancing the solar plexus chakra, you will have enough self-control, self-respect, self-worth, self-love, and enough of resilience and physical stamina. Also, a balanced chakra helps a person to make the major decisions of his life confidently, which ensures his success in the long run. When there is a blockage or any disturbance in this chakra, you might experience anxiety, a feeling of inadequacy, and indecisiveness. It is very important to rebalance this chakra, which can be done through meditation in particular. Remember that if the solar plexus chakra is overactive, it can make a person very aggressive and overbearing. You need to keep it balanced so that it will not affect your mind as well as your body negatively.

4. The Heart Chakra (Anahata)

The fourth chakra in your body is referred to as the heart chakra. This chakra acts as a gateway between your higher and lower chakras. This chakra is considered to be the gateway to the soul, particularly in classic yoga texts. It is also called the primary heart center. This chakra is located directly above your heart. The color associated with the heart chakra is green, and the element linked to it is air. This chakra also acts as a bridge between your mind, body, and soul. When everything is well with this chakra, or it is balanced, a person will be able to be emotionally open. He will also be able to be empathetic towards others and will be able to enjoy a very deep sense of his inner peace. Also, he will be able to understand his emotions on a cognitive level and will feel them fully. Any negative thing related to love will disturb this chakra, such as a grief process, a breakup, any casual cruelty, and a difficult friendship. A blocked heart chakra will result in many emotional issues and behaviors. When this chakra is misaligned or blocked, a person will struggle a lot to relate to other people. He may be impatient in different situations and will be less compassionate. He will not show any empathy to other people. People whose heart chakra is blocked are usually not at peace with themselves, and they find it extremely hard to trust other people. They will feel disgruntled and restless. A blocked heart chakra can also cause many physical issues. According to some chakra experts, a misaligned or blocked heart chakra can be linked to low immune system function and high blood pressure.

Summary sheet of the Heart Chakra

- Position: in the center of the chest
- Color: green
- Function: compassion, love, generosity, humility, openness to others
- Element: air
- Sense: touch
- Mantra: Yam, O
- Stones: All green stones, in particular, Aventurine and Tourmaline
- Lotus: 12 petals with two inverted triangles in the Centre forming a 6-pointed star
- Note: fa
- Animal: Antelope

The heart chakra, or the fourth chakra, is the most central chakra. It unites the lower chakras, which are more material chakras with the higher chakras, which are more spiritual. This chakra is closely related to the circulatory system, heart, lungs, chest, and heart plexus. When this chakra is open, you will be able to love others unconditionally and will be able to be more generous with other people. Also, you will be able to be very heartfelt and caring. As far as the physical aspect is concerned, air will be able to enter your lungs more fluidly. Your lungs will be filled with oxygen, which will then be transported to the rest of the body with the help of your circulatory system. There are many problems associated with a closed heart chakra. The first major problem is that when your heart chakra is blocked, you will not be able to love yourself as well as the people around you. You will be very apathetic and cold. Thus, its interactivity will make you a suspicious person; you will not be able to trust people easily. Other consequences linked to the malfunctioning of this chakra include cardiac and respiratory diseases, inability to love, disconnection, selfishness, and isolation. Thus, there is a need to rebalance your heart chakra whenever it is misaligned or blocked.

A person's heart chakra is connected to all of the following emotions:

- His capacity for empathy
- His emotional openness
- The intensity he cares for others
- Self-reflective capacities
- Self-knowledge
- How peaceful he feels

The blockages in your chakras can be major or minor, leading to various physical and emotional issues. Some of the major symptoms of a blocked heart chakra include lack of empathy, irritability, restlessness, impatience, increased blood pressure, insomnia, immune system dysfunction, etc. At times you will not be able to know the cause of misalignment or blockage of your heart chakra. Experts claim that one of the major causes which lead to heart chakra blockage is difficult relationships. These relationships are not necessarily romantic; even toxic friendships can disturb your heart chakra.

5. The Throat Chakra (Vishuddha)

The fifth chakra is known as the throat chakra, which is located in the middle of your throat. This chakra plays a key role in regulating a person's self-expression in all senses. The throat chakra influences how authentically a person coveys his deepest self to the outer world. An individual's emotional honesty, ownership of needs, directness, etc. are linked to the throat chakra. The color associated with this chakra is blue, and the element linked to it is ether. When a person's throat chakra is balanced, he will be able to speak to others properly and will be well understood by the people around them. In addition, he will be able to speak the truth appropriately. A person with an open and balanced throat chakra will be forthright and will not be blunt. There can be a disturbance in your throat chakra if you encounter difficult experiences with communication, such as a bad argument or a tough job interview. The blockage in your throat chakra will lead to certain emotional issues and behaviors. The first major issue is that a person whose fifth chakra is blocked will not be able to say what he really wants to say. A person might feel as if he is stuck holding onto secrets. In addition, a person may feel that the people around him are not interested in listening to his thoughts and that he is not able to find the appropriate words or language to express or convey his feelings. The blockage in the throat chakra can be major or minor. When there is a major blockage or misalignment, a person will experience discomfort in the throat, hormone fluctuations, and pain in the neck.

Summary sheet of the Throat Chakra

- Position: In the middle of the throat
- Color: light blue
- Function: listening communication, opening to others
- Element: ether
- Sense: hearing
- Mantra: ham, E
- Lotus: 16 petals with a triangle in the center with the tip pointing downwards
- Note: sol
- Stones: lapis lazuli, aquamarines all blue stones, especially sodalite and chalcedony
- Animal: white elephant

The throat chakra controls your neck, hands, arms, throat, and is also associated with cervical plexus or the bronchial. The color of the throat chakra is light blue, and it symbolizes transparency. When it is open, a person can express himself openly and transparently without offending anyone. You will feel that your voice is relaxed and calm. When it is open, you know how to listen to others around you properly, and you will be able to say whatever you want. In addition, our ability to concentrate enhances, and our learning becomes effective and fast.

On the other hand, the closure of the throat chakra makes a person feel extremely awkward and shy, and he cannot express his creativity well either through artistic disciplines or through words. All this results in great discomfort. The interactivity of this chakra also results in many physical issues such as asthma, mouth ulcers, bronchitis, earaches, and speech disorders. When this chakra is overactive, a person becomes logorrheic. He will never listen to what others say to him. Thus, there is a need to keep this chakra balanced as it's under, and overactivity leads to serious consequences. In this case, a person will not be able to say what he thinks, and his conversations will be based on manipulations and lies. He will not be able to accept criticism from others even from his closed ones because such a person feels too self-confident. When your throat chakra is unbalanced, all you need is to start learning to appreciate listening and silence. You also need to bring out your creativity.

Another important thing to remember is that your throat and crown chakra pair up together in your body. You need to ensure the good functioning of the throat chakra as it is crucial to heal or open the crown chakra. Salamba Sarvangasana is one of the major ways to keep your fifth chakra balanced.

6. The Third Eye Chakra (Ajna)

The sixth important chakra in your body is known as the third eye chakra or simply the sixth chakra. It is located at the center of our brow. The color associated with this chakra is indigo, and the element linked to it is extra-sensory perception. When this chakra is working well, it becomes a very powerful source of energy. This chakra determines a person's ability to see the bigger picture of his life. Also, it also determines our intuition and our alignment with this universe. When it is open, a person will be able to adept at picking up signs.

Moreover, he will be able to trust his gut feelings and will plan according to his greatest goals in life. Manifestation experiences and the law of attraction successes also relate to the openness of a person's third eye chakra. The third chakra can be misaligned or blocked if someone makes you doubt your own wider purpose. There are many problems associated with a blocked or misaligned chakra. The first major issue is that when a person's third eye chakra is blocked, he might feel that there is no point in what he is doing. He may feel that whatever he does is insignificant. Also, he may be struck by his inability to make decisions in life. Some people refer to this state as a feeling of psychological paralysis. In addition, a person might feel clumsy and may have trouble sleeping.

Summary Sheet of the Third Eye Chakra

- Location: In the middle of the forehead (between the eyebrows)
- Color: indigo or purple
- Function: foresight, intuition, imagination,
- Element: light
- Sense: sixth sense, sight
- Mantra: om, aum, I
- Stones: Amethyst, labradorite, fluorite, moldavite, lapis lazuli, opal, zircon, sodalite, sapphire
- Note: la
- Lotus: 2 petals with a triangle in the middle with the tip downwards
- Animal: The symbolism does not involve a representative animal for the third eye chakra

The third eye chakra is connected to your eyes, forehead, brain spinal cord, and temples. In addition, all duality and opposites are connected in this chakra, such as good and bad, form and substance, body and mind, reason and intuition, male and female, etc. It is very important to keep this chakra open or balanced because when it is blocked, a person becomes cynical, selfish, cold, calculating, and materialistic. In case it is blocked or misaligned, you will only believe in what you see with your eyes and will not be able to perceive what exists beyond. In addition, you will become very detached and insensitive and will no longer plan for your life ahead or dream. You will lose the ability to stay focused and concentrate on something for a longer period.

Moreover, there are certain physical issues associated with blocked or misaligned chakra such as headache, migraine, insomnia, fatigue, eye pain, neurosis, blindness, etc. Remember one thing that at times this chakra can be overactive or too open. In that case, a person becomes more self-celebrating, and he tends to blame other people for his faults. Thus, you need to make sure that this chakra is not closed as well as not too open. Try to keep it balanced, only then you will be able to maintain your inner serenity and stable relationships with other people. There are different ways through which you can rebalance your third eye chakra. One of the most important ways is meditation.

7. The Crown Chakra (Sahasrara)

The seventh important chakra in your body is referred to as the crown chakra. This chakra is also called the head heart center. The crown chakra is located at the top of your head. This chakra has the highest frequency among all the chakras in the body. The color associated with this chakra is violet, and the element linked to it is thought. This chakra is polarized negatively and is feminine in nature. The seventh chakra is the highest chakra, and it determines our spiritual connectivity. This chakra is vital to attain a feeling of peace as well as to establish a life you love. When everything is well with this chakra, or it is balanced, a person will be able to experience feelings of love and joy. He'll be in tune with the beauty in the world around him. To such a person, life will feel glorious, rich, and worthwhile. Remember that any traumatic experience in life may move this chakra out of positive, which causes a person to doubt himself and his purpose. There are certain emotional issues and behaviors which are associated with the blocked or misaligned crown chakra. The first major issue is that when this chakra is disturbed or blocked, a person will not be able to see or observe the beauty of this world. He may experience various symptoms of anxiety or depression and will feel spirituality adrift. Also, he may also experience a decline in his overall motivation or excitement.

Summary Sheet of the Crown Chakra

- Position: above the head
- Color: deep purple, white
- Function: knowledge, pure awareness or universal awareness
- Element: Metal
- Stones: diamond, hyaline, amethyst, quartz
- Sense: empathy and thought
- Mantra: ah, om, I
- Note: Yes
- Lotus: a thousand symbolic petals indicating infinity with a light in the middle
- Animal: The symbolism does not have a representative animal for the crown chakra

The crown chakra controls the top of your head, the brain, and the nervous system. This chakra is linked to the enlightenment as well as the energy of the universe. The opening of the crown chakra gives a person tranquility, happiness, well-being, and wisdom. We will be compassionate, understanding, and patient. In case the energy flow of the crown chakra is blocked, you won't be able to cultivate your spirituality. You will feel depressed, despondent, apathetic, and unwilling to live. If this chakra is too open or overactive, you will be attached to many unimportant things, power, and material goods. In addition, you will be overwhelmed by dissatisfaction and ignorance, and you will always feel arrogant, impatient, and anxious. The overactivity of this chakra will also lead to certain physical issues in your body; you will suffer from depression, mental confusion, exhaustion, and schizophrenia. Moreover, problems with the crown chakra will develop many negative features in your personality; you may develop a very high ego, rigidity in thinking, materialistic values, bullying, wanting to be right all the time, etc. Thus, there is a need to keep this chakra balanced. One of the ways which might help you to rebalance your crown chakra is "yoga positions."

Ways to Clean and Heal your Chakras

As we discussed the seven important chakras in your body, namely, Root Chakra, Sacral Chakra, Solar Plexus Chakra, Heart Chakra, Throat Chakra, Third Eye Chakra, and Crown Chakra. These chakras begin from the bottom of your spinal cord to the top of your head. It is important to keep these chakras clean and to heal them whenever required. Various techniques can clean and heal your chakras. Some of the fantastic ones include:

1. **Meditation**

    The first major technique to clean and heal the chakras is the chakra meditation. We will discuss the steps for the seven chakras one by one.

    Root Chakra: Remember that in all meditation, the first thing you need to do is find a very comfortable place keeping your back straight. This is vital in the process of healing all of your chakras. After finding such a suitable place, you need to close your eyes and start deep belly breathing. For beginners, it is recommended to lie down and breathe through their nose to ensure that they are doing it correctly. After practicing belly breathing in this position for a few days, you can sit up if you are comfortable with it. One thing that you need to notice is as you inhale the air, your belly fills first and then your chest. Take deep breaths via your nose and make sure that there is no separation between inhalation and exhalation. You have to do this for at least five minutes, and as you are breathing, you need to be aware of your body. The easiest way is concentrating well on the breath as it goes in & out. Make your breathing more rhythmic and allow it to become deeper. With every breath, you will feel more and more relaxed.

The second step is putting attention on your root chakra (first chakra), which is located at the base of the spine. Imagine that you're breathing in and out via your root chakra. When you inhale, the air will go down to the base of your spine, and when you exhale, it will go up through your nose without any separation between your breaths. As you exhale, you need to sense or visualize that the energy in your root chakra grows stronger via this chakra meditation. Since this chakra as a fiery red ball that is growing stronger and brighter with each exhale. Allow your consciousness to move down your energy ball. Visualize yourself as the ball of energy drawn towards the earth.

The third step is as you are doing the above steps, you need to focus on how you feel mentally, emotionally, and physically. Pay deep attention to what you experience as you are doing the steps. This step is quite difficult for most people. Few people even have experienced cycles of the earth or imagery with the earth, birth and death, and a partnership linked with Mother Earth. Meditation with the root chakra enables a person to get in touch with various aspects of his earth-like nature as well as his interdependent relationship and connection with the earth.

You need to do this part for almost ten minutes or until you feel satisfied. After that, when you are fully prepared to return to the room, you have to say, "Every time I reach this relaxed state, I learn to use my mind more creatively and become more aware of energy blocks that have kept me a prisoner so that I may heal myself." Then you have to release the energy ball and the imagery. After that, start counting from 1 to 5, feeling relaxed, peaceful, and refreshed as you go back to the room and start opening your eyes.

Sacral Chakra

Remember that for every chakra, there are different types of chakra meditation steps that you need to follow. The sacral chakra is also referred to as the sexual center. The first step for this chakra would be the same as the root chakra. After following the first step, you need to put your attention to the sacral chakra, which is located above the genitals in the public area, just about 3 inches below your navel. Visualize that you are inhaling and exhaling via your sacral chakra in the body. As you breathe in, the air will go down to the sexual organs, and while exhaling, it will go up via the nose without any separation between breaths. Visualize that on each exhalation, the energy in the sacral chakra grows stronger. Imagine your second chakra as an orange ball, which is growing stronger and brighter as you exhale. Allow your consciousness to move down into the ball of energy. Imagine becoming the ball and imagine or sense if you have started to radiate towards the outer side from that center via your body and later on into the outside environment. You also need to feel the sense of wonder and magic that radiates from your sacral chakra via meditation.

The third step involves paying attention to how you feel emotionally, mentally, and physically as you are doing the above steps. You also need to be aware of what you are experiencing at that particular moment. Remember that it is different for every individual. Some of you might feel a spontaneous burst of energy that runs up and down your spine or through your body. When you experience such a situation, you do not have to panic because it is normal, and you need to enjoy it. Some of you might feel them as vibrations or warm current of energy running through your body. Such sensations show an increased energy flow in your body. During this time, you need to pay attention to the changes you are experiencing. You should not try to influence these changes. Rather, just carefully observe them.

Meditating on the sacral chakra will enable a person to get in touch with various aspects of his sexuality and the creative process. You need to do this for at least ten minutes or till the time you feel satisfied. After a while, as you realize that you are ready to return to the room, you have to say "Every time I reach this relaxed state, I learn to use my mind more creatively and become more aware of energy blocks that have kept me a prisoner so that I may heal myself." Release the imagery and the ball of energy, and you need to count from 1 to 5 feeling peaceful, relaxed, and refreshed as you open your eyes. Thus, these are the major steps that you need to follow to clean and heal your sacral chakra (second chakra).

The Solar Plexus Chakra

The third important chakra in your body is the solar plexus chakra, which is situated around the stomach area at the top of your abdomen.

The first step for the solar plexus chakra would be the same as for the above chakras. The second step would be putting your attention on the solar plexus chakra in your body. As you breathe in, the air will go down to this chakra, and as you breathe it out, it will go up through your nose without any separation between breaths. As you exhale, you have to visualize energy in the solar plexus chakra growing stronger. During meditation with this chakra, visualize or imagine a yellow gold ball that is growing stronger and brighter with every inhale. Allow your consciousness to move down to this energy ball. Imagine becoming the ball and imagine or sense if you have started to radiate towards the outer side from that center via your body and later on into the outside environment. Once you do this, you will feel as if you have started to melt.

All this will be followed by a next step where you need to focus on how you feel emotionally, mentally, and physically. You also need to be aware of the changes you are experiencing. The moment your consciousness radiates from this center, you might feel yourself becoming more fluid and watery. Also, you might also feel deep empathy. This empathy is a product of contentment and trust. It will allow you to feel compassion for the suffering and pain of other people around you and also for yourself. You need to surrender to these feelings allowing them to flow through you.

You need to do this part for almost ten minutes, or till the time you may feel satisfied. The moment you are prepared to return to the room, you have to say, "Every time I reach this relaxed state, I learn to use my mind more creatively and become more aware of energy blocks that have kept me a prisoner so that I may heal myself." After that, you need to release the imagery and the ball of energy. Count from 1 to 5 feeling peaceful, relaxed, and refreshed as you open your eyes. Thus, these are the major steps you need to follow in third chakra meditation, which is needed to clean and heal it.

The Heart Chakra

The fourth chakra in your body is known as the heart chakra, which is located directly above your heart.

The first step for the heart chakra meditation would be the same as for the above chakras. If you intend to do just one chakra, you have to follow the first step, which is common for all the chakra meditation. On the other hand, if you intend to do all of them, you need to continue unchanged from the previous ones.

In the second step of the heart chakra meditation, you need to put all your attention on your fourth chakra. Visualize as if you are inhaling and exhaling through your heart chakra in the body. As you inhale, the air will go down to the heart chakra, and when you exhale, it will go up via your nose without any separation between the breaths. As you exhale, visualize that the energy in your heart chakra is growing stronger. During the heart chakra meditation, imagine an emerald green ball of light that grows stronger and brighter upon each exhalation. Allow your consciousness to move down into this energy ball. Imagine becoming the ball and imagine or sense if you have started to radiate towards the outer side from that center via your body and later on into the outside environment.

All this will be followed by a third step where you need to feel the supreme love, which is radiating through your heart and into the other chakras. As you are doing this, you need to focus on how you feel emotionally, mentally, and physically. The more a person is centered in the heart, the more he'll feel the mystic heart of Christ in him, which is referred to as Christ consciousness. The whole body starts pulsating with energy from the top of the head to the bottom of feet as the rivers of living water are radiating through your heart. When it happens, you will experience a warmth that throbs from the heart and will then fill your entire body. At this stage, you need to surrender to the energy which is emitting from your heart. By doing so, you will feel unconditional love for yourself and the people around you. You might experience that condition, which is explained by Jesus as "the peace that passes all understanding."

You need to do this part for almost ten minutes, or till the time you may feel satisfied. The moment you are prepared to return to the room, you have to say, "Every time I reach this relaxed state, I learn to use my mind more creatively and become more aware of energy blocks that have kept me a prisoner so that I may heal myself." After that, you need to release the imagery and the ball of energy. Count from 1 to 5 feeling peaceful, relaxed, and refreshed as you open your eyes. Thus, these are the major steps you need to follow in Fourth chakra meditation, which is needed to clean and heal it.

The Throat Chakra

The fifth chakra in your body is known as the throat chakra, which is located in the middle of your throat.

As discussed above, the first step for the throat chakra meditation would be the same as for the other chakras.

In the next step, you need to put your attention on the fifth chakra meditation. Visualize that you are inhaling and exhaling through the throat chakra. The air will go in and out via your throat without any separation between your breaths. As you exhale, visualize that the energy in the fifth chakra is growing stronger. During the throat, chakra meditation, imagine a glimmering blue ball of energy that is growing stronger and brighter upon every exhalation. Imagine becoming the ball and imagine or sense if you have started to radiate towards the outer side from that center via your body and later on into the outside environment.

These will be followed by a third step where you need to feel your character as noble, courageous, and fearless. At this stage, you need to be centered in your throat, which will enable you to feel more victorious. At every moment, you need to experience the honesty of choosing yourself. When doing so, your life will be more triumphant at each and every moment of your life without diminishing other people. Say this to yourself over and over; "At last I am free."

After experiencing the victory, you might feel streams of energy that shoot up your spine. These streams become currents of unconditional joy the moment they pass your throat. By accepting this victory, you will be able to fulfill the purpose of your life.

You need to do this part for almost ten minutes, or till the time you may feel satisfied. The moment you are prepared to return to the room, you have to say, "Every time I reach this relaxed state, I learn to use my mind more creatively and become more aware of energy blocks that have kept me a prisoner so that I may heal myself." After that, you need to release the imagery and the ball of energy. Count from 1 to 5 feeling peaceful, relaxed, and refreshed as you open your eyes. Thus, these are the major steps you need to follow in Fifth chakra meditation, which is needed to clean and heal it.

The Third Eye Chakra

The sixth important chakra in your body is known as the third eye chakra, which is located at the center of your brow.

The first step for the third eye chakra meditation would be the same as for the above chakras. If you intend to do just one chakra, you have to follow the first step, which is common for all the chakra meditation. On the other hand, if you intend to do all of them, you need to continue unchanged from the previous ones.

In the second step, you need to put all your attention on your third eye chakra (the sixth chakra in the human body). Visualize that you are inhaling and exhaling through the third eye chakra. The air will go in and out without any separation between your breaths. As you exhale, visualize that the energy in the sixth chakra is growing stronger. During the third eye, chakra meditation, imagine an indigo ball of light that is growing stronger and brighter upon every exhalation. Imagine becoming the ball and sense if you have started to radiate towards the outer side from that center via your body and later on into the outside environment.

All this will be followed by a third step where you need to feel like the union of selves. Also, visualize that your mind is radiating instantaneously in all directions. Imagine as you are filling the room with consciousness. While doing all, you need to pay attention to how you feel emotionally, mentally, and physically. The union of consciousness and unconsciousness will be complete if you are more centered in your sixth chakra.

An electric current will be produced during this condition, which will run through your entire body. As a result of this, your head glows.

You need to do this part for almost ten minutes, or till the time you may feel satisfied. The moment you are prepared to return to the room, you have to say, "Every time I reach this relaxed state, I learn to use my mind more creatively and become more aware of energy blocks that have kept me a prisoner so that I may heal myself." After that, you need to release the imagery and the ball of energy. Count from 1 to 5 feeling peaceful, relaxed, and refreshed as you open your eyes. Thus, these are the major steps you need to follow in Sixth chakra meditation, which is needed to clean and heal it.

The Crown Chakra

The seventh chakra in your body is known as the crown chakra, which is located at the top of your head. With the seventh chakra, meditation is not possible because people do not exist as separate beings.

You can easily activate awareness of feelings and emotional blocks through meditation on these chakras. For different people, these come in different ways. It depends on the spiritual gifts an individual might have already developed. Clearing and removing your energy blocks will enhance a person's spiritual gifts by making him stronger as well as by opening him to new abilities and awareness, which he might not be aware of previously.

All the seven chakras in your body provide you with some psychic gifts which are as follows:

i. The gift of the root chakra is gut feelings and unlimited intuition.

ii. The gift of the sacral chakra meditation is clairsentience (Clear feeling), the sensing of love, energy, ideas, etc.

iii. The gift of the solar plexus chakra is sensitivity to vibrations from places and people.

iv. The heart chakra's gift is enabling an individual to be empathetic with others mainly because he has traveled down the path, and now he sees others working through.

v. The throat chakra's gift is clairaudience (clear hearing). It involves hearing from the high vibrational levels to the inner ear words and ideas.

vi. The gift of the third eye chakra is clairvoyance (Clear seeing). It involves seeing such high levels of vibration forms that an individual cannot normally see with physical eyes like auras, visions, higher beings, and energies.

> vii. The crown chakra's gift is Ascension, the I AM and Cosmic Consciousness.

In conclusion, meditation with all these chakras is vital in the process of cleaning and healing them. The chakra meditation provides an individual with numerous benefits and ensures his well-being.

1. Affirmations

Other powerful tools that can be used for chakra healing include affirmations. These are the positive statements that heal and strengthen the damaged part of one's self. Working on these affirmations enables us to focus on different aspects. These are some examples of affirmations for the seven chakras in your body.

The Root Chakra or first chakra – "I am filled with humility. I am enough as I am."

The Sacral Chakra or second chakra – "I am radiant, beautiful and strong and enjoy a healthy and passionate life."

The Solar Plexus or third chakra – "I accept myself completely. I accept that I have strengths, and I accept that I have weaknesses."

The Heart Chakra or fourth chakra – "Love is the answer to everything in life, and I give and receive love unconditionally."

The Throat Chakra or fifth chakra – "My thoughts are positive, and I always express myself truthfully and clearly."

The Third Eye Chakra or sixth chakra – "I am wise, and I understand the true meaning of life's situations."

The Crown Chakra or the seventh chakra – "I am complete and one with the divine energy."

It is possible to use affirmations for each of the seven chakras if you wish. If you feel that there is something wrong with any one of them, then you have to focus all your energy on healing that particular chakra in your body. For example, if a person feels that his creativity is stifled, then he needs to focus on his second chakra or sacral chakra.

2. Massages for balancing

Another common technique that can be used for healing and cleaning the chakras is 'massages.' By massaging properly, you will be able to heal your chakras easily. Remember one thing that on each chakra you need to apply different massage methods such as:

The first or root chakra: For healing your root chakra, you need to massage your legs, feet, and gluteal muscles. Massaging in these specific parts will make the energy flow better in your body.

The second or sacral chakra: To heal or clean this chakra, you need to focus on releasing tension in your hip area. This can be done by releasing the iliopsoas muscle and myofascial release for the hip flexors.

The solar plexus or third chakra: In the case of this chakra, you need to massage around your belly button using oils in a clockwise direction. This will promote the functions of different organs in your body as well as promote the elimination of waste.

The heart or the fourth chakra: In case of the heart chakra, you need to massage your upper back, gently apply pressure to your arm, shoulder joint, pectoral muscles and myofascial.

The throat or the fifth chakra: In the case of the fifth chakra, you need to apply pressure to your neck. Also, you have to release the restricted fascia tissues which are located around your back and in the front of your neck.

The third eye chakra or the sixth chakra: In the case of the third eye chakra, you need to perform a technique which is referred to as brow stripping. In this technique, you massage the muscles in the nasal sinuses, jaw area, and temples.

The crown or the seventh chakra: This chakra massage involves releasing cranial tissue adhesions with cervical traction, scalp massages, and hair pulls.

Thus, with the help of proper massages on these chakras will enable you to clean and heal them.

3. Color Vibration

You can change your physical states, moods, and emotions by exposing yourself to different types of colors, having different vibrations. By exposing your body to different colors at your home, in your food, and the clothes you wear, you can easily heal the chakras in your body. There is another important way to absorb colors that are wearing color glasses. These glasses absorb the vibrations that are needed in your body. Remember that each chakra in your body is associated with a different color.

- The color associated with the root chakra is red.
- The color associated with the sacral chakra is orange.
- The color associated with the solar plexus chakra is yellow.
- The color associated with the heart chakra is green.
- The color associated with the throat chakra is blue.
- The color associated with the third eye chakra is indigo.
- The color associated with the crown chakra is violet.

In this way of chakra healing, we need to target our problem chakra by exposing yourself to the color associated with it. Make conscious choices at home décor, clothing, and diet. For example, if you feel that you are suffering from communication problems, then there is something wrong with your throat chakra. To heal it, you need to decorate your home or office in blue tones. By doing so, you will be able to expose your throat chakra to specific color vibrations.

4. Chakra Stones

Another important way to clean and heal your chakras is the "chakra stones," which are referred to as healing crystals. The chakra stones contain specific vibrations and colors. Each chakra in your body has a specified color associated with it. This color is used in the

process of Chakra healing. Mostly, a stone with a specified color is used to heal one particular chakra. However, some stones can be used for healing multiple chakras. One example of such stones is Clear quartz. A question that may arise in your mind is how actually to use these chakra stones? You simply need to place the stone in the area where your chakra is located. Also, you can wear these chakra stones as jewelry. While sleeping, you can also put them under your pillow or put them around your house. Thus, using the chakra stones, you can easily heal your chakras.

5. Yoga for Chakra Healing

Yoga is also an important way through which you can clean or heal your chakra. When the chakras are stuck or blocked, it is better to release the prana or energy using movement. One of the most beneficial and recognized techniques to release stagnant or stuck energy out of your body is 'yoga postures.' Different yoga postures will enable you to be fresh and vital energy back into your body. Thus, yoga is the major way that promotes the flow of energy in the body. Different postures and movements in yoga can expel negative energy from your body and unblock your chakras.

6. Music for Chakra Healing

Another important way for cleaning and healing the chakras in your body is 'music.' Each chakra in your body responds to various sound healing frequencies. One of the most popular techniques is Solfeggio, where different healing sounds are produced using music frequencies. Another popular technique is the Isochoric Chakra Suite, where the brainwave entertainment method is used. In the case of this technique, chakra healing is promoted by combining Tibetan singing bowls with Solfeggio frequencies. Thus, such type of music is very beneficial in healing and cleaning the seven chakras in your body.

7. Professional Energy Healers

Another amazing way to heal your chakras is 'professional energy healers.' Visiting a professional energy healer will be very beneficial for you if you ever come across a blockage in any of your chakras. These energy healers figure out why there is an energy blockage in your body by assessing your energy levels. By doing so, they will be able to locate the causes of energy blockages. After a thorough examination, these professionals offer you a suitable healing treatment for chakra cleansing or healing. You can easily heal any spiritual blockage by contacting or reaching for the right healer.

8. Essential Oils for Chakra Healing

Essential oils are also very important in the process of chakra healing. Generally, these oils are used in combination with different massage techniques. Few of the most recommended oils for the seven chakras in your body are as follows:

- Root Chakra or first chakra: Angelica, Frankincense, St. Johnís Wort, and Patchouli
- Sacral Chakra or second chakra: Clove, Neroli, Orange, Juniper, and Rosemary
- Solar Plexus or third chakra: Peppermint, Marjoram, Lemon, Rosemary, and Yarrow
- Heart Chakra or fourth chakra: Basil, Melissa, Rosewood, and Rose
- Throat Chakra or fifth chakra: Blue Chamomile, Lemongrass, and Sage
- Third Eye Chakra or sixth chakra: Lavender, Clary Sage, Elemi, and Spruce
- Crown Chakra or seventh chakra: Myrrh, Sandalwood, Geranium, and Gotu Kola

Thus, by using these essential oils either alone or in combination with various massage techniques, you will be able to clean or heal all of the seven chakras in your body.

Many people prefer to follow this method for chakra healing as they find it more easy and convenient.

Meditation for Chakra Healing

It is also possible to clean your chakras through meditation. To meditate properly, you need to follow certain steps, particularly when you are a beginner. These important steps are as follows:

I. First of all, you need to find a quiet and peaceful place where you can sit for about thirty minutes, and no one would bother you in the meantime.

II. The second step is sitting in a comfortable position in that particular place you have found for yourself. In this step, you need to sit with your legs closed. You can also sit in a cushion if you want. Remember that a comfortable position is vital in the process of chakra meditation. So, you need to sit comfortably wherever you desire.

III. In the third step, you need to sit up straight. Make sure that your spine is not too tense. In case it is too tense, it will be difficult for you to meditate properly.

IV. After that, you need to rest both the hands-on your knees comfortably.

V. In the next step, you need to inhale and exhale (breath in and out) slowly and steadily.

VI. The sixth step is very crucial, where you need to imagine all of your chakras as well as the energy that is flowing in and out of these chakras. At this stage, using the color associations will help you in visualization. Remember that each chakra in your body is associated with a different color; Root – red, Sacral – orange, Solar Plexus – yellow, Heart – green, Throat – blue, Third Eye – indigo, Crown – purple and white.

VII. In the seventh step, you need to focus on each of the chakras in your body for several minutes. At the end of this meditation, a person must have a good picture of the energy flow in his body.

VIII. You can also use guided meditation tools and techniques whenever you need them.

Thus, through proper meditation, you can clean your chakras. You need to dedicate meditation time for each of the seven chakras in your body, particularly if you are a beginner. In the initial meditation sessions, you might find it hard, but with time and practice, you will be able to have a good grasp on each of the seven chakras in your body. Meditation has proved to be very useful in the process of chakra healing. People prefer to meditate as it offers numerous other benefits along with chakra healing and cleansing.

In conclusion, chakra healing and cleansing is very important as there are many problems associated with blocked chakras. The most amazing ways to heal your chakras include meditation, affirmations, color vibrations, music, yoga, essential oils, etc.

How to Unblock Chakras?

In the previous chapters, we discoed in general what are the different ways to clean and heal the

chakras in our body. In this section, we will be looking at each chakra in detail and the ways to unblock them. The importance of unblocking the chakras can be understood through these examples; when you are going to work, and you see that the roads are blocked due to heavy traffic, you will not be to get to work on time. In the same way, if the chakras in your body are blocked due to various factors, your body will not be able to function properly. The first thing to understand here is, why do we experience blockages in our chakras? Various factors may contribute to chakra blockage. Keep in mind that blockages can be emotional, physical, spiritual, etc. In case of emotional blockage, the causes are mental illness like depression, anxiety or addiction, and emotions stored from your past. These are referred to as emotional residue or toxins. When we accumulate these in our body, they will result in blockage of the energy flow of your chakras. The blockage can also be physical such as a tumor, fatty deposits in your arteries, excess waste, and a cyst. There are various reasons due to which blockages are created in the physical body, such as lack of exercise, poor diet, overwork, overexertion, lack of sleep, and drug use. Also, these blockages can also be spiritual in nature.

They can come from the spiritual forces within us or from outside spiritual forces. You block your higher chakras by refusing to honor the spiritual side of who you are. If you are strict and rigid spiritually, you can restrict energy flow in your body. One thing that you need to be careful of is that these internal or external forces can create harm without your conscious awareness. Other than that, the blockages in your chakras can also come from your karma. Karma is a Sanskrit word that means action. During our life, we perform different kinds of actions; some actions are nourishing and good; some are harmful or bad, and some are neutral. Let's take the example of each type of action. A good action could be donating money to charity, a bad action may be deceiving someone or lying intentionally, and a neutral action is making the bed. You might have heard the phrases "As you sow so shall you reap" or "what goes around comes around." It is generally believed that if you do well in life, you will have good. On the other hand, if you do badly to other people, you will also suffer at some stage of your life. So these are a few of the major reasons due to which you may experience blockages in your chakras. Now, keeping in view the problems associated with the blocked chakras, we need to look at the ways through which we can unblock them. Let's discuss each chakra individually.

1: The root chakra

This chakra is foundational. When everything is okay with this chakra, we feel calm and secure. Also, we will be confident and bold enough to deal with the challenges of our life. Our root chakra needs to be properly aligned. Only then will we be able to try new things and pursue the goals of our life.

One more thing that we need to understand is what the root chakra is responsible for; when the root chakra is open, your mind, as well as your body, are optimized for success. On the other hand, a blocked or misaligned root chakra is associated with stagnation and unhappiness. This chakra is related to the basic needs of an individual's life. It is located at the base of our spine and is highly responsive to all the things that are connected to our security. For instance, the root chakra influences or is influenced by:

- How grounded a person feels
- Our basic needs such as shelter, food and rest
- Sense of safety a person feels
- Our survival
- How confident a person feels to grow and change

All these things mean that when the first chakra is properly aligned, a person will be at peace. You will be relaxed, comfortable, and stable with your life. In contrast, this chakra can be misaligned or blocked quickly if something in our life doesn't feel secure. For example, if we are worried about any basic needs such as money or housing, this will have a great impact on our first chakra.

There are certain symptoms of a blocked root chakra such as:

- Increase in the anxiety level in the body
- Feeling unsafe or threatened
- Panic attacks and panic attack symptoms such as a racing heart or hyperventilation
- Negativity towards others as well as towards yourself
- Difficulties in concentration
- A very unhealthy relationship with food such as binging, purging or starving
- A very low self-confidence
- You start doubting things that you initially used to take for granted
- You find it hard to make decisions
- Extreme reliance on external feedback
- Hypochondria

In addition to these symptoms, certain physical symptoms are associated with a blocked or misaligned chakra. Some of the symptoms include back pain, pain in legs, cold feet and hands, discomfort indigestion, and lethargy.

There are some cases when a person won't even know why his first or root chakra is blocked. One thing that you need to keep in mind is that your root chakra gets blocked by anything that will shake your sense of security. Some of the common examples from your daily life include failure in relationships, loss of a job, coming across financial difficulties, conflict with relatives, or close family members.

How to unblock the root chakra?

The opening of every chakra in your body has different benefits for our emotional and bodily well-being. Therefore, you need to develop various techniques to unblock your chakras so that your body would continue to function normally. By unblocking your root chakra, you will be able to experience a deep sense of comfort and relaxation. Also, you will develop your self-confidence. The following are a few of the techniques through which you can balance your root chakra.

Stones and jewelry to unblock the root chakra

Unique stones can be used to influence the chakras in your body and to unblock them. You can use these stones in the form of jewelry as well. Simply by holding the stones and wearing the jewelry, you can unblock or realign your blocked chakras. Remember that each chakra in your body is associated with a different stone. Various traditional stones are used in healing the root chakra; the first major stone is Red Jasper.

As you know that the root chakra is associated with red color, so most of the stones that are used in unblocking the root chakra are usually red. This stone plays a key role in balancing your root chakra. Another important stone that is used to unblock your root chakra is Red Carnelian, which is pale red and has orange hues. This stone is associated with bravery, cleansing, and strength. This stone is useful, particularly when a person is unable to bring himself to get out of his comfort zone and when he is struggling with fearfulness. Obsidian is also a traditional stone which is black and is known to protect us from harm. Wearing this gemstone, we will be able to draw some comfort as we are working to move to a more secure place in our life. Another famous stone is the Bloodstone, which is green in color. This stone has red spots on it; perhaps this is the reason it is named as bloodstone. This stone is famous for increasing the confidence of a person as well as for pushing away the negative energy in the body. This is known to be the perfect stone to deal with or combat with a misaligned or blocked root chakra. Thus, by using these stones or wearing them as jewelry, you will be able to unblock your first chakra.

Yoga and meditation techniques to unblock root chakra

Another important technique that helps unblock the root chakra is 'yoga and meditation.' The meditation techniques used here are similar to the regular meditation technique, but here you need to focus on that particular part of the body where there is something wrong. One of the simple but most effective techniques of root chakra meditation is as follows:

In the first step, you need to sit with your spine straight and your shoulders back. As you breathe deeply and close your eyes, try to keep all your muscles relaxed. Breathe in through your nose, pull the breath as far down to the body as you possibly can, and the breath out through your mouth. In the second step, you need to draw all your focus and attention to the root chakra, which is located below the tailbone. You have to notice if there is any tightness in this particular area. As the color associated with this chakra is red, so you need to visualize a red glow or a red ball of energy at the base of the spine. Slowly, this glow will expand, which will make the whole area relaxed and warm. You need to stay in this sensation for about 3-5 minutes. After 3 or 5 minutes, you have to open your eyes slowly. Before continuing your routine or day, you need to sit for a few minutes.

As far as the yoga techniques are concerned, the most famous yoga pose that helps unblock the root chakra is Balasana. In this pose, you lay with your face down resting on calves and knees, as your head drops down you extend your arms out in front of you until your head is between them. Try this pose if you are struggling with the misaligned root chakra. Meditation and yoga techniques are used by the majority of the people as they find it easy and more convenient. Also, these techniques are very beneficial for the overall well-being of an individual.

Diet suggestions and Foods' list for chakra healing

It is also possible to deal with the chakra blockages by taking a proper or recommended diet. Just that you need to make minor changes in your diet. Experts who are working on opening and rebalancing the chakras are very much interested in finding the impact various food can have on the well-being of your chakras and their alignment. The first thing you will find is that a healthy diet will surely help you to unblock your chakras and to keep them balanced. It means that you need to increase the intake of vegetables and fruits and reduce the levels of saturated fats, sugar, and salt.

Remember that there are specific foods that are associated with your first chakra, such as organic foods. Eating any organic food will help you in the opening of the root chakra because this chakra can be opened by anything that is connected to your tribal roots. Also, you need to consume food that is rich in proteins. Protein-rich foods will boost your emotional strength by giving you more physical strength. Some good examples of protein-rich food include almonds, beans, spinach, green peas, and tofu. Thus, if you are struggling with blockages in your root chakra, you have to intake the foods that are rich in protein.

Moreover, red foods are also known for automatically influencing your first chakra because of the association of this chakra with the red color. Red foods give you a lot of Vitamin C, which is a bonus. Red bell peppers, tomatoes, cherries, and strawberries can be good options. In addition to red foods, red vegetables can also play a key role in unblocking the root chakra. Potatoes, garlic, and beets are common examples. Thus, you can align your blocked root chakra by consuming a proper diet.

Affirmations to use for healing the root chakra

The root chakra can also be unblocked using certain types of affirmations. Affirmations are positive statements. The following are the most commonly used affirmations in root chakra healing.

- "I am secure and happy in my home."
- "Wherever I am, I am safe and secure."
- I feel my root chakra opening, and I feel myself stabilizing."
- "I am stable, grounded, and relaxed at this moment."
- "The universe will always provide for me."
- "I have a healthy body, a healthy mind, and an abundant life."
- "I deserve and receive support whenever I need it."
- "The universe will always support me and show me where to go next."

2. The sacral chakra

It is the second chakra in your body, which is located in the center of the abdomen. This chakra is associated with your imagination, sex drive, the potential for personal growth, etc. When this chakra is misaligned or blocked, you will feel uninspired, listless, and bored. Also, you will also resist the changes in life and will have a very low sex drive.

You also need to understand what the sacral chakra is responsible for. The sacral chakra is influenced by the following:

- How inspired a person feels?
- An individual's ability to be playful with other people
- A person's satisfaction and happiness in a romantic relationship
- How much pleasure does a person feel in all spheres of his life?
- The self-confidence of a person
- Feedback on artistic things

So these are a few of the things which your sacral chakra influences and is influenced by. So, when the second chakra is open, a person will feel stimulated, full of ideas, and dynamic. The proper alignment of this chakra will also give you the confidence to make the major changes in your life.

Symptoms of a blocked or misaligned sacral chakra

Like all the other chakras, the root chakra can also make you feel physically and emotionally destabilized. Some of the common symptoms include:

- Jealousy
- Boredom
- Getting offended easily
- Lacking creative inspiration
- Guilt of past
- Fear of change

- Addictive behaviors such as drug addiction, gambling, overeating, sexual compulsions, etc.

Apart from these, there are some physical symptoms as well, such as allergy symptoms, low energy, bladder discomfort, and reduced libido. You cannot possibly figure out the causes of blockage in the sacral chakra. However, the commonly known causes include reproductive health issues, sexual incompatibility, rejection of a person's creative input, rejection from someone you love, etc.

How to open your sacral chakra?

As discussed above, there are various problems associated with a blocked sacral chakra. So there is a great need for opening and unblocking it. By opening the sacral chakra, you will be able to enhance your self-esteem, to be engaged with other people, to let go of your past guilt, and will develop healthy ways to regulate your emotions. Also, you will also experience the profound inspiration and will be able to enjoy each and every moment of your life. Your problem-solving skills will be more refined if your sacral chakra is open. Below are the most powerful techniques which can be used to open a blocked sacral chakra.

Stones and jewelry to unblock the sacral chakra

Some specific stones can be used for healing the sacral chakra. One of the most famous stone is Orange calcite. As you know that the second chakra is associated with the color orange, so the stones used in the process of healing this chakra are also orange in color. This stone is known for enhancing your creativity. It also helps to overcome the emotional barriers and reunite body and mind. Another important stone is the Moonstone, which comes in various colors. However, people prefer opting for peach moonstone because it is famous for stimulating your mind. This stone carries a kind of loving energy and also reduces worry. Carnelian is also a semi-precious gemstone that is used in the process of healing the sacral chakra. Although it comes in different shades, it has a reddish-brown hue. Being the Singer stone, it is known to be the perfect stone for healing the sacral chakra. This stone has an intrinsic link with a person's artistry and creativity. Another major stone is Citrine, which is golden yellow. Sometimes, these stones are also referred to as stones of the mind. This stone plays a key role in increasing your self-esteem.

Yoga and meditation techniques to unblock a sacral chakra

Yoga and meditation techniques are also very useful in unblocking the sacral chakra. The steps of meditation for this chakra healing are similar to the ones followed in the standard meditation practice. However, the visualization component is involved in this chakra meditation. The following are the steps that you need to follow in sacral chakra meditation.

In the first step, you need to find a quiet and comfortable place where no one can disturb you. While doing so, you have to keep the spine straight, and the limbs relaxed. After this step, you have to take ten deep and slow breaths. Visualize a spinning orange circle or ball in the place where your sacral chakra is located. As the elements associated with the sacral chakra is water, so you have to visualize that this energy ball is spreading out in the form of rippling waves. Feel that your body is warming up as a result of this. You need to do this for about five minutes, after which you have to open your eyes slowly when you are ready.

Yoga practice is also very helpful in aligning the sacral chakra. Dvipada Pitham is the most common posture for sacral chakra healing. In this posture, you need to lie on your back and lift your hips. At the same time, you have to lift your arms over your head. This is known to be the best sacral chakra yoga pose. Thus, through meditation and proper yoga practice, you will be able to align your blocked or misaligned sacral chakra.

Diet suggestions and Foods' list for sacral chakra healing

Each chakra in your body responds either positively or negatively to the food you eat. It is possible to unblock this chakra simply by making little changes to diet. A healthy diet will always be very helpful in opening the chakras in your body. However, certain foods are linked to the sacral chakra historically. Some of the common sacral chakra foods are:

Oranges: As we discussed earlier that the sacral chakra is associated with the color orange, so this fruit surely has a connection with it. Remember that any fleshy fruit you eat will help you to keep your sacral chakra open and aligned, such as peaches, papayas, and mangoes.

Seeds: In addition to the fruits, certain seeds play a key role in aligning the sacral chakra. You can eat some of the good seeds, such as sunflower, hemp, poppy, and pumpkin.

Coconuts: Coconuts are an amazing choice if you are dealing with issues with the second chakra, such as low inspiration. Coconuts are famous for increasing the energy level and getting a person into the right mood to be active and creative. Thus, they can be used for aligning the sacral chakra.

Teas and broths: Clear liquids are commonly known to heal the sacral chakra. So, fruit tea or a tasty vegetable broth can be a good choice if you are struggling with chakra healing.

Thus, to deal with the sacral chakra issues, you need to start a healthy eating plan.

Affirmations used for healing the sacral chakra

In addition to the above techniques, various powerful affirmations can also be used to unblock or heal the sacral chakra. Affirmations are positive statements that can be used for chakra healing purposes. Few of the most common and powerful affirmations are as follows:

- "I am full of inspiration and the potential for creation."
- "I am ready for positive change and deep personal growth."
- "I deserve to experience pleasure and have my needs met."
- "It is safe to express my sexual self in fun, creative and healthy ways."
- "I am confident that what I offer the world is enough."
- "I know I can embrace change and make the best of my future."
- "I attract relationships with loving, good people who will support me."
- "My body is vibrant, and I am comfortable inside it."
- "Every day, I experience more and more joy and satisfaction."
- "I am a strong, creative person, and I love what I create."

To sum up, the sacral chakra can be healed or aligned through meditation, yoga, healthy diet, and affirmations. Proper alignment of this chakra is vital for the proper functioning of your body.

How to unblock the solar plexus chakra?

The third chakra is your body known as the solar plexus chakra, which is located around the stomach at the top of the abdomen. A properly aligned or open chakra will enable you to see things clearly and to make good decisions in your life. Also, you will be able to refine your self-concept and will boost your confidence to a great extent. When everything is good in life, we will surely feel good about ourselves. When this chakra is blocked, our confidence becomes very shaky. We will also come across numerous self-esteem problems, will have trouble with memory and digestive discomfort. Keeping in view these problems, we need to keep the solar plexus chakra balanced.

Various factors can impact your solar plexus chakra. Some of which are as follows:

- How a person responds to criticism from others
- Whether an individual sees himself as "good enough."
- A person's capacity of self-forgiveness
- Self-discipline
- Whether a person learns lessons from the difficulties he encounters in life
- An individual's independence
- How a person defines himself and the purpose of his life

Thus, a properly aligned solar plexus chakra ensures how a person feels self-assured, certain of his own identity, as well as sure of what he needs to do to be successful in life. Remember that the solar plexus chakra can be misaligned by any sudden change you encounter in your life. It can also be blocked by the things that undermine you or by the difficulties you may come across while moving on from your past mistakes. You also need to remember the fact that the overactivity of this chakra is also not good for your health, as it can result in feelings of anxiety or mania. Thus, you need to make sure that your solar plexus chakra is not underactive and overactive; it should be balanced.

Symptoms of a blocked or misaligned solar plexus chakra

There are certain symptoms associated with a blocked or misaligned solar plexus chakra. Some of the most common symptoms include:

- ❖ Feeling helpless
- ❖ Feeling as if we need to control everything and everybody around us
- ❖ Finding it difficult to see the big picture of life
- ❖ Low self-esteem
- ❖ Lack of direction or purpose
- ❖ Feelings of guilt about past

If you encounter a minor blockage in your solar plexus chakra, then just you will lose confidence. Other areas of your personality will not be impacted. However, if the blockage is bigger, you will experience lower self-esteem, and at times you will also feel that you are a worthless being. In addition to the above symptoms, certain physical symptoms are associated with a blocked solar plexus chakra such as nausea, digestive cramps, bloating, and difficulties with your short-term memory. Thus, if you are experiencing any of these symptoms, you need to start working on your solar plexus chakra to open or balance it.

How to open your solar plexus chakra?

As we discussed above that there are various problems associated with a blocked solar plexus chakra. Working on this chakra will provide you with numerous benefits. You will be able to boost your confidence and will also reduce procrastination.

Stones and jewelry to unblock the solar plexus

Different stones can be used in several ways for chakra healing purposes. You can simply carry these stones in your pocket, can keep them in your palm while meditating and can wear them as jewelry. The following are the stones that are associated with the solar plexus chakra:

Amber: As the solar plexus chakra is associated with the color yellow so the amber stone being orangey-yellow is used in the process of healing this chakra. These stones are linked to mental clarity and confidence. Using this stone will be beneficial for an individual who is struggling to make a decision in his life.

Yellow tourmaline: This stone is physically striking and can often be seen advertised as a detox stone. Using this stone will help you to get rid of negativity about the past and yourself.

Citrine: This is another pale yellow stone that is used to heal the solar plexus chakra. Sometimes this is also referred to as the success stone. This stone can be used to increase personal empowerment and to develop your self-esteem.

Yoga and meditation techniques to unblock solar plexus chakra

The solar plexus chakra can also be healed using yoga and meditation techniques. The steps followed in the solar plexus chakra meditation are:

After finding a comfortable and quiet place to meditate, the first thing you need to do is to turn your attention to the solar plexus chakra, which is located in the upper abdomen. After that, you need to visualize a yellow ball of energy in the center of your upper abdomen. Concentrate slowly in making this energy ball brighter and wider. As this ball grows to imagine as if it is rotating in a clockwise direction. As you do so imagine this area of your body becoming more relaxed and warmer. You need to do this for about three to five minutes. After that allow this energy spread throughout the body, you need to take a few deep breaths and then slowly open your eyes.

In addition to meditation, yoga can also help heal the solar plexus chakra.

The common yoga pose associated with the solar plexus chakra is as follows: firstly you need to put a cushion or a soft blanket under your knees. Then kneel and sit on your heels. Move the knees to make them hip-width apart. Now kneel so that your torso sits between the thighs.

Diet suggestions and Foods' list for solar plexus chakra healing

As we discussed earlier that through a healthy diet, we could heal the chakras in the body. The particular chakra foods that speed up the process of solar plexus chakra healing are as follows:

Yellow peppers: You can add yellow peppers to your diet if you are struggling with your solar plexus chakra is the color associated with this chakra is yellow.

Corn: Corn is also an amazing choice to heal this chakra. It can give an extra boost to your well-being and can nourish your solar plexus chakra. In a beginner's guide to chakras, this food is often mentioned first.

Complex Carbohydrates: The complex carbohydrates can give you a steady energy supply. So, they can be used for healing or unblocking the solar plexus chakra. Few examples of complex carbohydrates include wholegrain cereal, brown bread, and brown rice.

Chamomile tea: Chamomile tea is also recommended to deal with a blocked solar plexus chakra. This tea can settle an unsettled stomach.

Thus, by adding the above food to your diet, you can easily heal your solar plexus chakra.

Affirmations used for healing the solar plexus chakra

Along with the above techniques, various affirmations are also used to heal the solar plexus chakra. Affirmations are positive statements that are known to boost your self-esteem and self-confidence. These positive statements can reduce the blockages in your solar plexus chakra. Some of these affirmations are:

- "I am the embodiment of inner peace and confidence."
- "We don't need to be in control of everything in our lives."
- "I'm powerful, and I am comfortable with that power."
- "I have high self-esteem and feel better about myself every day."
- "I feel motivated to pursue my purpose."
- "I'm ambitious, capable, and ready to fulfill my purpose."
- "I release myself from negative past experiences."
- "I know I am worthy, good, and capable."
- "The only thing I need to control is how I respond to situations."
- "I forgive myself for past mistakes, and I learn from them."

Thus, you can try one or even more of these affirmations to deal with the blockages in your solar plexus chakra.

How to unblock the heart chakra?

The fourth chakra in your body is known as the heart chakra, which is located directly above your heart. When this chakra is properly aligned, we will be more compassionate with other people. On the other hand, a blocked heart chakra will make you less compassionate and impatient. You will find it extremely hard to trust other people and will not feel at peace. Thus, it is important to keep this chakra balanced to ensure your overall well-being.

Many experts say that this chakra acts as a bridge between your emotions, thoughts, and spirituality. It is connected to the following things:

- A person's capacity for empathy
- Self-knowledge
- An individual's intensity to care for others
- Self-reflective capacities
- How peaceful a person feels

Symptoms of a blocked or misaligned heart chakra

The blockages in your heart chakra can be major or minor. They will lead a person to feel emotionally or physically off balance. There are various symptoms associated with the blocked heart chakra. Some of which are as follows:

- Lack of empathy with other people
- Difficulty in trusting others
- Restlessness
- Irritability and impatience

In addition to these, there are also some physical symptoms of a blocked or misaligned sacral chakra, such as increased blood pressure, insomnia, and a decrease in the function of the immune system. At times you may not know what is wrong with this chakra. However, it isn't necessary to know the cause to heal this chakra. Experts claim that one of the major causes could be difficult relationships. These relationships do not need to be romantic ones; even toxic friendships can play a role in blocking your heart chakra. These problems could be an incompatibility with your partner, end of a relationship, etc. Whatsoever is the cause a blocked or misaligned heart chakra is harmful to your physical as well as emotional health. Thus, there is a need to keep this chakra open and properly aligned.

How to open your heart chakra?

As we discussed earlier that there are various problems associated with the blocked heart chakra. Therefore, we need to look for the techniques through which this chakra can be healed. If this chakra is open, you will be able to meet and understand your needs in a much better way. The following are a few of the approaches which you can try to open your heart chakra:

Stones and jewelry to unblock the heart chakra

The chakra stones are very easy to use. You can simply hold them in your hands while meditation or can wear their jewelry. As you know that the color associated with the heart chakra is green, therefore most of the stones used for healing this chakra are green in color. Some of the most common stones are:

Jade: This is a semi-precious stone that is linked to emotional healing and balance. While dealing with an emotional injury or loss, you can use this chakra stone. It will benefit you to a great extent.

Green calcite: This is another important stone used to heal the heart chakra. This stone has been used to absorb negativity traditionally. When you find it hard to feel empathy, this stone will be an excellent choice for you.

Green aventurine: This stone is mostly linked to inspiration, vitality, and energy. This stone helps in bouncing back from various emotional roadblocks. It also soothes difficult emotions.

Rose quartz: This stone is pink in color and sometimes referred to as the heart stone. It can help a person to regain balance.

Thus, using these stones, you will be able to align your heart chakra, which is vital for your physical and emotional well-being.

Yoga and meditation techniques to unblock the heart chakra

If you are learning to align or unblock your chakras, it is a good choice for you to practice various yoga and meditation techniques daily. Mindfulness exercises such as body scanning and deep breathing can play a role in the proper alignment of your chakras. However, there are also some specific yoga and meditation techniques to practice for the heart chakra healing. One of the best meditation techniques for the heart chakra is as follows;

First of all, you need to find a relaxing and comfortable place where no one will be able to bother or disturb you. After finding such a place, sit there, and then you need to inhale through your nose and exhale through the mouth. Do this for a couple of minutes, and while doing so, you need to feel your body relaxing. Imagine green energy that starts at the base of your spine and moves up in your body towards your heart. Visualize that this energy is turning into a solid green ball. As you breathe in and out, imagine the ball of energy becoming brighter and bigger. In the next step, you need to put your attention on the feelings of love for other people as well as for yourself. Allow this green energy to radiate throughout the body. You need to practice this meditation technique for about three to five minutes.

Diet suggestions and Foods' list for heart chakra healing

The heart chakra can also be healed by adding certain foods to your diet. The best foods that you can consume when your heart chakra is blocked are as follows:

Green Foods: As mentioned above that the color associated with the heart chakra is green. So the green foods are the best choice to heal this chakra. For example, green apples, spinach, limes, kale, green bell, peppers, etc. These foods can help you in balancing your heart chakra.

Foods that are rich in vitamin C: In addition to the green foods, the foods that are rich in vitamin C are also a good choice for heart chakra healing. Fruits such as strawberries, oranges, and other fruits are high in vitamin C and thus can be used to heal this chakra.

Warm soups: Warm soups can surely help a person recover from difficult experiences and replenish his emotional stores. These soups can also help in speedy recovery.

Affirmations used for healing the heart chakra

The heart chakra can also be unblocked using affirmations, which are positive statements. Affirmations are very helpful in building confidence as well as getting old and limiting beliefs. Some of the good affirmations used to heal the heart chakra are:

- "I choose joy, compassion, and love."
- "My heart is free from all the wounds of the past."
- "I love myself unconditionally, and offer the same love to others."
- "I know my own emotions, and I accept whatever form they may take."
- "I forgive others, and I forgive myself."
- "I am open to love and receive more of it every day."
- "Every day, I fulfill my heart's desire."
- "I give love freely, and it brings me joy."

- "I create supportive, loving relationships that are good for me."
- "My heart chakra is open, and I am well."

Thus, you can try one or even more of the above affirmations to heal your heart chakra. Say them every day to deal with the blockage in the chakra.

How to unblock throat chakra?

The fifth chakra in your body is known as the throat chakra, which is located in the middle of your throat. Like all the other chakras, this chakra also needs to be balanced or healed. When everything is well with this chakra, a person will be great at making himself understood. He will be able to say with tact whatever he wants to say. The proper alignment of this chakra is essential for your personal as well as professional life.

On the other hand, there are many emotional issues and behaviors associated with a blocked or misaligned throat chakra. Firstly, you will not be able to say what you wish to say. Also, you will not be able to find the right words to express yourself or your feelings. All of this will lead to emotional discomfort, which will affect your overall well-being. Thus, there is a need to keep it balanced.

In addition to this, we also need to understand what the throat chakra is responsible for. Various factors in the body are affected by a blockage in the throat chakra. Some of which are:

- ❖ A person's emotional honesty
- ❖ Whether a person lives an authentic life
- ❖ How well a person handles confrontation or conflict
- ❖ The quality of an individual's relationship
- ❖ A person's ability to be heard
- ❖ Awareness of one's needs

Symptoms of a blocked or misaligned throat chakra

It is normal for you to experience blockages in your throat chakra now and then. There are various symptoms associated with a blocked or misaligned throat chakra. Some of which are as follows:

- You will find it difficult to say what you want to say
- You will feel as you lack vocabulary or words to express your emotions
- You will also feel as if you are holding onto secrets in your life
- You will develop a sense that the other people around you are not aware of the 'real you.'

In addition to these symptoms, there are certain physical symptoms as well that are associated with a blocked or misaligned throat chakra. Such as:

- Achy or stiff neck
- Fluctuations in the level of hormones in your body
- Sore throat

If you are experiencing these symptoms, then you surely need to consider them and start working on your throat chakra. There can be various causes due to which the throat chakra gets misaligned, for example, a negative or cruel appraisal at work, harsh words being said to you by someone during an argument, etc. Moreover, if you have a habit of keeping your feelings to yourself or being secretive, you are more likely to develop blockages in your throat chakra.

How to open your throat chakra?

Different approaches are used by experts to open your throat chakra. Some of which are:

Stones and jewelry to unblock the throat chakra

As discussed earlier, various stones and jewelry are very beneficial for chakra healing purposes. The color associated with the throat chakra is blue, so most of the stones and jewelry used to heal this chakra are blue in color. It is very easy to use these stones. You can carry them in your bag, can hold them in your hands while meditating or can wear them as jewelry. Some of the most popular throat chakra healing stones are as follows:

Lapus Lazuli: This is semi-precious stones, which is also referred to as the stone of truth. So, this is an ideal stone if a person is trying to communicate honestly.

Amazonite: Another major stone used for healing the throat chakra is amazonite. It is a turquoise stone that is very helpful in protecting a person against negativity. So, if you feel that you are unable to be honest in life, you have to try this stone.

Aquamarine: This is one of the most famous chakra stone crystals. This stone represents acceptance and courage. You can try this stone if you feel that you are having communication problems in your close relationships.

Turquoise: It is also a famous semi-precious stone that is well-known for the throat chakra healing. This stone is popular for increasing your confidence in communication.

So, by carrying these stones with you or by wearing their jewelry, you will be able to deal with your blocked or misaligned throat chakra.

Yoga and meditation techniques to unblock the throat chakra

In addition to the above techniques, the throat chakra can also be unblocked using different meditation and yoga techniques. Throat chakra meditation needs to be done daily for about ten minutes. You will be able to see effective results even if you practice meditation just a few times a week. You need to follow the following steps if you are struggling with a blocked throat chakra:

First of all, you need to find a comfortable and quiet room for yourself where no one could disturb you. In this room, you have to sit in a comfortable chair. Then you need to breathe in and breathe out as deeply as you can ten times. You need to inhale through your nose and exhale through the mouth. In the next step, you need to start scanning from the top of your head down your body. While doing so, imagine the muscles in your body relaxing. After doing this for the whole body, you need to visualize a spinning blue ball. You need to see this ball sitting at the level of the throat. Imagine as if it is glowing and become brighter. Imagine that the energy ball is growing bigger & bigger. After that, you need to focus on a feeling of relaxation and openness in your throat chakra. Let this energy spread throughout your body and then slowly open your eyes when you feel that you are ready.

You can also try certain yoga poses to open the throat chakra, such as supported fish pose, cobra pose, and shoulder stand.

Diet suggestions and Foods' list for throat chakra healing

Certain chakra foods are known for promoting the overall balance and openness of your chakras. Just by making some minor dietary changes, you can deal with the blockages in the chakras. The following are the foods that are used particularly to heal the throat chakra:

Blueberries: Blueberries are one of the most common foods used for healing the throat chakra. To make a delicious healing smoothie for this chakra, blueberries can be mixed with coconut and blackberries.

Whenever you feel that you are having challenging conversations, you can try this food. Blueberries will be very beneficial for you in the process of throat chakra healing.

Simple spices: If you are trying to heal your throat chakra, then you need to add lemongrass, ginger, and salt to the food you consume. By doing so, you will be able to promote self-expression.

Fruits that grow on trees: Traditionally, all the fruits that grow on trees, such as oranges, apples, etc., are associated with the throat chakra. The reason is that they symbolize authenticity. These fruits fall from the trees only when they are fully ripe and ready to eat.

Thus, it is easy to open or align your throat chakra simply by adding the above foods to your diet. You can consider adding one or many of these foods to get better results. The bonus of adding these foods is that they are very healthy for your mental as well as physical health and have no side effects. Thus, these foods will promote your overall well-being and will make your life worth living.

Affirmations used for healing the throat chakra

Along with the above techniques, various affirmations are also used to heal the throat chakra. Affirmations are positive statements that are known to boost your self-esteem and self-confidence. These positive statements can reduces the blockages in your throat chakra. Some of these affirmations are:

- "I am always understood by others."
- "My voice is important in this world."
- "I can vocalize my emotions, no matter what they are."
- "I honor my true voice, and I let it speak."
- "When I speak, my contributions are honest but balanced."
- "I am an empathetic listener and a clear communicator."
- "I can find the right words in all situations."
- "I speak my true thoughts with ease."
- "Others hear my voice."
- "Let go of doubt about the word I 'should' have said."

Simply by trying these affirmations, you will be able to heal the throat chakra.

To sum up, the throat chakra can be unblocked using stones and jewelry, yoga and meditation techniques, specific foods, and affirmations. The proper alignment of the throat chakra is vital for the well-being of both your body and mind.

How to open the third eye chakra?

The sixth chakra in your body is known as the third eye chakra, which is located in the center of the brow. This chakra is connected to our spirituality. When this chakra is open or when everything is well with this chakra, we will be able to use both logic and feelings to make the major decisions of our life. Also, we will be able to trust our intuition and will be well aware of the purpose of our life. On the other hand, if the third eye chakra is closed or blocked, we will come across many emotional issues and behaviors. We will not be able to make good decisions and will start doubting our abilities and the overall purpose of our life. Also, you may also feel clumsy, will have trouble sleeping as well as will struggle to learn new things in life. Keeping in view all these problems associated with a close third eye chakra, it becomes essential for us to keep it open or balanced. Experts use numerous approaches to heal a blocked third eye chakra. Some of the most common ones will be discussed ahead.

Here we also need to understand what the third eye chakra is responsible for? It is responsible for or is influenced by the following things:

- ❖ A person's ability to form precise gut feelings
- ❖ An individual's sense of the bigger picture of his life
- ❖ Whether a person meets goals related to his deepest purpose
- ❖ Balancing Reason and emotion
- ❖ Whether a person feels he is moving forward or is stagnant

So, all these things are influenced by or influence the third eye chakra in your body.

Symptoms of a blocked or misaligned third eye chakra

You need to detect the symptoms or signs of the third eye chakra blockages. Once you detect them well, you will be able to deal with them. Some of the major symptoms associated with a blocked or misaligned third eye chakra include:

- ❖ Paranoia
- ❖ Finding your life or work insignificant
- ❖ Indecisiveness
- ❖ Feeling pointless
- ❖ Lacking faith in your purpose

In addition to them, there are certain physical symptoms which are associated with blockages in this chakra. Such as:

- ❖ Sinus pain
- ❖ Leg and back pain
- ❖ Eye discomfort
- ❖ Headaches

Thus, these are few of the symptoms or signs which show a blockage in the third eye chakra. You also need to be aware of the causes of the blockages. There are various things or incidents that can push your third eye chakra out of alignment. For example, when a person belittles your passion or vocation. Likewise, transitional life experiences such as job loss, divorce, death, illness, etc., can also block your third eye chakra. When you are aware of the symptoms as well as causes, it will be very easy for you to deal with the problems in your chakras.

How to unblock the third eye chakra?

As we use certain techniques to heal or unblock all the other chakras in the body, the same would be done for the third eye chakra. Some of the major techniques used by experts are as follows:

Stones and jewelry to unblock the third eye chakra

The color associated with the third eye chakra is indigo, so most of the stones used in third eye chakra healing will also be indigo in color. You can use these stones in any of the ways you are comfortable with. For example, you can simply carry them in your bag; you can hold them in your hands while meditating or wear them as jewelry. Certain stones are associated, particularly with the third eye chakra healing. Some of which are:

Black Obsidian: This is a common crystal used for third eye chakra healing. This stone has a role in promoting a balance between reason and emotion.

Purple fluorite: This is another semi-precious stone which is known for clearing up jumbled thoughts as well as promoting sharpened intuition. If you are trying to get rid of various irrelevant distractions or trying to make any difficult choice in life, then this stone would be an ideal choice for you. It will help you in making good choices and decisions in your life.

Amethyst: Another famous and precious stone used for healing the third eye chakra is amethyst. It is known historically to be used against headaches. People also use this stone to represent wisdom.

Healing the third eye chakra using stones is quite an easy process as you do not need to struggle much. Many people prefer using this technique to heal their third eye chakra as they find it more easy and convenient in comparison to the other approaches.

Yoga and meditation techniques to unblock the third eye chakra

Another major technique through which the third eye chakra can be healed is 'yoga and meditation.' You can start with the following meditation, particularly if you are a beginner.

First of all, you need to find a quiet place and sit there comfortably. Close your eyes and then breathe in and out ten times, deeply and slowly. After that, you need to put your attention on the area where your third eye chakra is situated. Visualize a violet sphere of energy. As you continue breathing slowly and deeply, visualize as if this energy ball is getting warmer and bigger. While doing so, imagine that this ball is purging negativity from the body. Think as if you are absorbing the energy of the third eye chakra. Let yourself feel this all over. After doing this, when you feel that you are ready, then you have to open your eyes.

This meditation technique is quite easy and is very useful, particularly for beginners. You can practice it a few times a week. You will be able to deal with the blockages in your third eye chakra simply by practicing this meditation technique.

In addition to meditation, yoga is also very helpful in the process of third eye chakra healing. The most famous and beneficial yoga poses for healing this chakra are the eagle pose and the child pose.

Diet suggestions and Foods' list for third eye chakra healing

In addition to the above techniques or approaches, the third eye chakra can also be healed by a specific diet plan. There are specific foods that are known to promote third eye chakra healing. Some of which include:

Dark chocolate: If you are trying to heal your third eye chakra, you can consume as much as the dark chocolate as you can. The dark chocolate is famous for boosting concentration and enhancing mental clarity. It is rich in magnesium, which distresses you. Also, this chocolate has a role in promoting the release of serotonin.

Omega-3: Foods that contain omega-3 play a key role in enhancing your cognitive functions and, thus, in keeping your third eye chakra open. Some of the foods that are rich in omega-3 include sardines, chia seeds, salmon, and walnuts.

Anything purple in color: As we discussed earlier that the color associate with the third eye chakra is purple; thus, all the foods that are purple in color will help you to keep this chakra open and balanced. Examples of such foods include blackberries, blueberries, red grapes, purple cabbage, and eggplant.

Thus, you can unblock your third eye chakra simply by adding some specific foods to your diet. Remember that healthy foods such as vegetables, fruits, whole-grain foods, and healthy fats are known to promote the overall balance and openness of all the chakras in your body. However, with each particular chakra, certain specific foods are associated traditionally. You need to study all the chakras and foods associated with them to deal with the blockages or misalignments. Chakra healing will be easier for you if you have a thorough knowledge of all the techniques used for healing purposes.

Affirmations used for healing the third eye chakra

Affirmations are also very helpful in the process of healing the third eye chakra. These are the phrases or statements that target limiting and negative beliefs and then replace them with positive beliefs. Affirmations can help a person in so many ways, from finding love to weight loss. Perhaps this is the reason they are used in the chakra healing process. While designing affirmations for your third eye chakra, you need to focus on your gut instincts and spirituality. Some of the most common affirmations used in third eye chakra healing are as follows:

- "My third eye is open and ready to see my purpose."
- "I know how to make the right decisions, and I do so with ease."
- "I follow the lead of my inner teacher."

- "I hear my intuitions, and I know they will lead me to my purpose."
- "I live every day in accordance with my life's purpose."
- "I am on my true path."
- "I trust the guidance that my third eye gives me."
- "I am an intuitive person, and I know what is right for me."
- "I have unlimited possibilities available to me."
- "It is safe and good to follow the guidance of my third eye."

How to open the crown chakra?

The seventh or the last chakra in your body is known as the crown chakra, which is located at the top of your head. When this chakra is fully open and properly aligned, a person will experience a lot of pleasure in his life. Also, he will feel alive, grateful, and will be able to enjoy his life to the best. On the other hand, if the crown chakra is misaligned or blocked, you will face many emotional issues and behaviors. If this chakra is blocked, a person will not be able to see the beauty in the world around him. He will also experience various symptoms of depression as well as will feel his spirituality adrift. With the blockages in this chakra, a person will feel a decline in motivation or excitement. Thus, it is important to keep the crown chakra open and balanced.

The following are the things the crown chakra is influenced by:

➤ Excitement levels of a person

- A person's ability to find peace
- How much beauty a person can see in the world around him
- An individual's motivation to accomplish the goals in his life
- Whether a person has a restful sleep

Symptoms of a blocked or misaligned crown chakra

As we discussed various problems associated with a blocked or misaligned crown chakra, now we need to understand the symptoms or signs that are associated with the blocked crown chakra. The crown chakra can be either overactive or underactive. Symptoms for both these conditions would be different from each other. Such as:

Symptoms of an overactive crown chakra include apathy, self-destructive tendencies, cynicism, disconnecting from spirituality, etc. On the other hand, symptoms of an underactive crown chakra include lacking inspiration, being confused about what you wish to do in your life, and a desire of oversleeping. In addition to these symptoms, there are various physical symptoms which are associated with a blocked crown chakra such as; exhaustion, chronic headaches, poor coordination, etc.

You also need to understand the causes of the crown chakra blockages. A few of the major causes could be negative feedback or criticism from people, a mid-life crisis like reevaluating your relationship or job and conflicted relationships. No matter what is the cause of crown chakra blockages, you have to learn to heal it.

However, knowing the cause and detecting the symptoms will make the overall process of healing easier for you.

How to unblock the crown chakra?

Like all the other chakras in your body, the crown chakra also needs to be balanced and open as its closeness can lead to serious problems in the body. Experts use numerous techniques to deal with the blockages in this chakra. In this section, we will discuss a few major ones among them.

Stones and jewelry to unblock the crown chakra

As discussed earlier that the color associated with the crown chakra is violet, so most of the stones or jewelry used for healing this chakra will be violet in color. When it comes to using stones for chakra healing, there are plenty of options; you can wear them as necklaces, bracelets, rings, or simply carry them in your bag. These stones will help you to open and align your crown chakra.

Some of the major stones that are associated specifically with the crown chakra include:

Sugilite: This is one of the major stones used for crown chakra healing. This stone is known as a love stone. It is used to guard you against negativity and for spiritual grounding.

Clear quartz: This is a crystalline mineral that is known for enhancing energy in the body. This stone can be used to boost spiritual attunement. If a person wishes to get clearer about what he wants from his life, this stone would be the best choice for him.

Selenite: This stone is also very popular in chakra healing processes. It has a role in healing both the crown chakra and the third eye chakra. This stone would be very beneficial for you to get rid of your past stagnations and moving forward.

Thus, you can try one or more of these stones to heal your crown chakra. Most people find this approach very easy and convenient, as they do not need to put in great efforts. Simply by wearing jewelry or carrying the stones in their bags, they can easily deal with the blockages in their crown chakra.

Yoga and meditation techniques to heal the crown chakra

Another useful technique used in the process of healing the crown chakra is 'yoga and meditation.' Remember that the meditation practices are good for all of your chakras. However, for each chakra, you need to follow a specific practice.

The following are the steps that you need to follow in crown chakra meditation.

First of all, choose a quiet and peaceful place for yourself. Sit comfortably with your foot on the floor and the back straight. Then you need to put both your hands in the lap and then turn your palms up to the sky. This position is referred to as the mudra, which is very helpful for receiving energy. In the next step, you need to close your eyes. Breathe in through your nose and out through your mouth. Then you need to imagine that there is a lotus at the top of the head. Breathe evenly and slowly, and as you do so, see the petals of the lotus unfurling for showing you a bright violet light, which is the color associated with the crown chakra. Imagine that this light is getting brighter, thus making the crown of your head warm. Allow this warmth to spread in your whole body. You need to do this for about five to ten minutes. After that, open your eyes and, for a few minutes, sitting quietly in that place. This meditation practice is very helpful, particularly for beginners.

In addition to meditation, various yoga poses are also very helpful for healing the crown chakra. Some of the most famous ones include; the seated lotus position, the supported headstand, and the plow. Simply by using these yoga positions, you will be able to align or balance your crown chakra. Yoga and meditation techniques are used widely by people all over the world. It is because these techniques are not just helpful for chakra healing but the overall physical and mental well-being of an individual. So, if you come across blockages in your crown chakra, you can try one or even more of these meditation techniques and yoga positions.

Diet suggestions and Foods' list for crown chakra healing

As you know that a healthy diet is vital for your mental as well as your physical health. Interestingly, a good diet can also promote the chakra healing process. Simply by making a few dietary changes, you can deal with the blockages in your crown chakra. If you are coming across blockages in any of your chakras, then you need to start consuming more vegetables, fruits, and healthy fat. These foods will help you to align your chakras. Try to avoid fattier foods. However, traditionally there are specific foods that are associated with the crown chakra. Some of which include:

Ginger: Ginger is a very healthy food when it comes to chakra healing. It is known to promote spiritual clarity and has cleansing benefits. Thus, you can add this food to your diet if you are struggling with the problems in your crown chakra.

Violet foods: All the foods that are violet in color will be beneficial for crown chakra healing because the color associated with this chakra is violet. Some of the best examples include red grapes, eggplant, and passion fruit.

Herbal teas: Herbal tea is also a good option for crown chakra healing purposes. It can reduce blockages in your crown chakra. One of the best choices could be peppermint, which is also helpful for the process of digestion.

Thus, it is possible to heal the crown chakra by adding healthy food to your diet and by cutting sugary or fatty food from your diet. If you are struggling with blockages in your crown chakra, then you must add the above foods to your diet. A healthy diet, along with a healthy lifestyle, will make your life worth living.

Affirmations used for healing the crown chakra

Along with the above techniques, various affirmations are also used to heal the crown chakra. Affirmations are positive statements that are known to boost your self-esteem and self-confidence. They replace negative and limiting beliefs with positive ones. These positive statements can reduce the blockages in your crown chakra. Some of these affirmations are:

- "We are all on this earth to make a difference."
- "I am constantly connected to my highest self."
- "I am attuned to the divine energy of the universe."
- "Today, I am open to divine guidance."
- "I know my own spiritual truth, and I live in accordance with it."
- "I see the beauty in the world, and I embrace it."
- "Lovingly, I emit light that attracts others who will bring love into my life."
- "I am at one with the world around me."
- "I am love, I am light, and I am joy."

- "Right now, I am confident, happy, and sure of my worth."

You need to add some of the above affirmations to your daily routine. Say these affirmations at different times of the day a few times. Simply by repeating them to yourself, you will be able to heal your blocked or closed crown chakra.

To sum up, the crown chakra can be healed with the help of jewelry and stones, yoga and meditation techniques, healthy foods, and affirmations. Before trying any of these approaches, you need to have proper knowledge of them.

Summary

If any of the chakras in your body is overactive or underactive, you will come across many issues. You need to understand this for each chakra:

Problems associated with an overactive root chakra

- Insecure
- Fearful
- Ungrounded
- Nervous
- Materialistic or greedy
- Resistant to change

Problems associated with an underactive root chakra

- Unable to feel at home or secure anywhere
- Codependent
- Fearful of abandonment
- Not being able to get into one's body

Problems associated with an overactive sacral chakra

- Overemotional
- Attracted to drama
- Very quick to attach and invest in other people
- Lacking personal boundaries
- Moody

Problems associated with an underactive sacral chakra

- lacking self-worth or self-esteem
- Stiff
- closed off to others
- Unemotional
- possibly being in an abusive relationship

Problems associated with an overactive solar plexus chakra

- Domineering
- Angry
- Aggressive
- overly critical of others or oneself
- Perfectionistic

Problems associated with an underactive solar plexus chakra

- Passive
- Timid
- Indecisive
- lacking self-control

Problems associated with an overactive heart chakra

- Loving in a suffocating, clingy way
- willing to say yes to everyone and everything
- lacking a sense of self in any relationship
- letting everybody in
- lacking boundaries

Problems associated with an underactive heart chakra

- Cold
- Lonely
- Distant
- unwilling or unable to open up to other people
- grudgeful

Problems associated with an overactive throat chakra

- Overly talkative
- highly critical
- unable to listen
- condescending

- verbally abusive

Problems associated with an underactive throat chakra

- Introverted
- Shy
- unable to express your needs
- Finding it difficult to speak the truth

Problems associated with an overactive third eye chakra

- Out of touch with reality
- unable to focus
- lack of good judgment skills
- susceptible to hallucinations

Problems associated with an underactive third eye chakra

- Rigid in thinking
- too reliant on authority
- closed off to new ideas
- distrustful or disconnected of the inner voice
- anxious
- fearful of the future
- clinging to the past

Problems associated with an overactive crown chakra

- neglectful of bodily needs

- Addicted to spirituality
- Finding it difficult to control your emotions

Problems associated with an underactive crown chakra

- Not being open to spirituality
- lacking direction
- unable to maintain or set goals

Thus, these are the major problems associated with underactive or overactive chakras. Keeping in view these problems, it becomes vital for us to deal with them so that we may not encounter more complications ahead. For beginners, it is also important to know about the endocrine gland and organs associated with the seven chakras in your body. Moreover, we will also look at the symptoms linked to blockages in the chakras.

Endocrine glands and organs associated with the root chakra

- Adrenal glands
- Blood
- Spine
- reproductive organs

Physical symptoms of an unbalanced root chakra

- Not being able to sit still
- unhealthy weight (either eating disorders or obesity)
- Restlessness

- cramps
- constipation
- fatigue
- sluggishness

Endocrine glands and organs associated with the sacral or second chakra

- Kidneys
- reproductive organs
- uterus
- ovaries and testes

Physical symptoms of an unbalanced sacral chakra

- Lower-back pain
- urinary issues
- Stiffness
- infertility
- kidney pain or infection
- impotence

Endocrine glands and organs associated with the solar plexus or third chakra

- digestive system (stomach and intestines)
- Central nervous system

- liver
- metabolic system
- pancreas

Physical symptoms of an unbalanced solar plexus chakra

- Ulcers
- Nausea
- Gas
- other digestive problems
- asthma or other respiratory ailments
- eating disorders
- nerve pain or fibromyalgia
- infection in the kidneys or liver
- other organ problems

Endocrine glands and organs associated with the heart or fourth chakra

- immune system
- Thymus gland
- heart
- breasts
- lungs
- arms
- hands

Physical symptoms of an unbalanced heart chakra

- Heart and circulatory problems (heart palpitations, high blood pressure, heart attack)
- asthma or other respiratory ailments
- poor circulation or numbness
- breast cancer
- joint problems in the hands
- stiff joints

Endocrine glands and organs associated with the throat or fifth chakra

- Thyroid
- Throat
- Neck
- Shoulders
- Mouth
- Ears

Physical symptoms of an unbalanced throat chakra

- soreness or stiffness in the shoulders or neck
- laryngitis or hoarseness
- sore throat
- infection or earaches

- thyroid issues
- dental issues or TMJ

Endocrine glands and organs associated with the third eye or sixth chakra

- Pituitary
- Brow
- Eyes
- base of skull
- biorhythms

Physical symptoms of an unbalanced third eye chakra

- Vision problems
- sleep disorders or insomnia
- headaches or migraines
- nightmares
- seizures

Endocrine glands and organs associated with the crown or seventh chakra

- pineal and pituitary glands
- Brain
- cerebral cortex
- Hypothalamus
- central nervous system

Physical symptoms of an unbalanced crown chakra

- Dizziness
- mental fog
- Confusion
- neurological disorders
- schizophrenia or other mental disorders
- nerve pain

When we have a thorough knowledge and understanding of all the above factors, it will be easier for us to heal and balance the chakras or energy centers in our bodies. Chakra blockage is not something that can be ignored; rather, it needs special consideration, and the problems need to be dealt with.

How to Practice the Chakra Balancing and Activating Meditation?

All the chakras in your body need to be balanced. There are numerous ways through which the chakras can be balanced or healed. Various meditation and yoga techniques are very useful when it comes to chakra healing.

Balancing and healing the chakras via Fire Breath

Fire Breath is very rejuvenating, relaxing, and healing for all the chakras as well as your energy body. This needs to be done in the following way;

First of all, we need to drop all other expectations and put ourselves in the energy state and mindset of the feeling which we desire. We need to let go of any expectation or attachment regarding the outcome. Next, we need to lie on the floor with the feet flat and our knees up. We have to relax our jaw and have to inhale through the nose and breathe out through the mouth. While doing so, we need to imagine that our breath is filling our belly like a balloon. As we breathe out, we need to flatten our lower back to the ground or floor. As we do this, there must be a gentle rocking in our pelvis. As we breathe out, we have to squeeze our Kegels. In the next step, as we inhale, we have to visualize pulling energy from the first chakra. We do not need to pull or push the energy; it'll simply follow our thoughts. Then, we need to inhale the energy from the first chakra up to our second or sacral chakra. Then we have to exhale, circulating this energy back down to the first chakra. Continue breathing in so that the energy moves between your root and sacral chakras. Keep repeating it until you feel that the energy is moving between these two chakras.

In the following step, we need to enlarge this energy circle by breathing healing energy from our first chakra up to our third chakra (solar plexus chakra). As we breathe out, we need to squeeze your Kegel muscles. We need to keep doing this several times. We have to reduce the circle when this feels complete so that the energy could move between our sacral chakra and our solar plexus chakra. As we continue breathing and squeezing our Kegels, we need to enlarge this energy circle so that it could move between our sacral chakra and the solar plexus chakra.

We need to keep repeating this for all our chakras letting the energy move throughout our body.

Conclusion

The seven chakras in your body are; the root chakra, the sacral chakra, the solar plexus chakra, the heart chakra, the throat chakra, the third eye chakra, and the crown chakra. Each chakra is located in a specific position in your body, and with each chakra, a specific color and element are associated. For example, the color associated with the root chakra is red, and the element is earth. For the sacral chakra, the color is orange, and the element is water. For the solar plexus chakra, the color is yellow, and the element is fire. For the heart chakra, the color is green, and the element is air. For the throat chakra, the color is blue, and the element is ether. For the third eye chakra, the color is indigo, and the element is extra-sensory perception; and for the crown chakra, the color is violet, and the element is thought.

Charkas interact with the energetic and physical body through the nervous system and the endocrine system. The chakras are associated with the endocrine glands in the body. They are also associated with plexus (a particular group of nerves). Thus, it can be said that each one of these chakras corresponds with specific parts of the body and perform specific functions that are controlled by an endocrine gland or the plexus. This is the key to understand how chakra healing methods work.

In addition to representing physical parts of the body, chakras also represent parts of our consciousness. All our possible states of awareness, perceptions, and senses can be categorized into seven different categories, which can be associated with any one of these chakras. For example, if a person feels stress in his consciousness, he will feel it in the chakra that is associated with that particular part of his consciousness experiencing the tension or stress. Likewise, when a person is hurt in a relationship, he will feel it in his heart. When a person is nervous, his legs tremble, and his bladder becomes weak. Whenever there is stress or tension in a specific part of our consciousness or the chakra associated with it, the nerves of the plexus detect the tension, after which it is communicated to different parts of your physical and energy body. When this stress or tension continues for a longer period, certain physical symptoms are produced, thus requiring the chakra healing to resolve. The physical symptom leads to an imbalance in the energy of your body. Therefore, there is a great need to reverse it. It can be reversed via physical change and chakra healing practices. This tension can also be released by changing your ways of being. In this way, you will be able to return to your natural state of health and balance.

Chakra healing is very crucial. Each chakra is connected to the nervous system and an endocrine gland in your body. So, if you ignore the energy deficiency for a long time, it can lead to severe physical consequences. The most important key in chakra healing is "balance."

It cannot be said that one particular chakra is important than the other. All the seven chakras in your body are important as far as the chakra healing and balancing is concerned. For example, a person cannot have low extra throat chakra energy and less heart chakra energy. It is not at all like that. All of the seven chakras in your body must be balanced, open, healed, and humming. Only then will they be able to transfer energy into your body or out of your body to the external world. One of the most important features of your body is that even if one of your chakras is underactive or closed, any other chakra may be overactive or open to manage the difference. If anyone of our chakras is overactive or underactive, it can have very negative impacts on the body. Therefore, our body always tries to maintain an energetic balance in all our chakras. The energetic imbalance can be counterproductive in the chakra healing process. When one chakra gets knocked out of balance, it can lead to an imbalance in any other chakra that may pull extra energy away from that particular part of the body. Thus, there is a need for balancing and healing.

The root chakra is foundational. When everything is well with the Root Chakra, you will feel anchored, calm, and secure in reality. You will be able to handle difficulties and tackle challenges boldly. While doing so, you will feel very confident. The Root Chakra is very important whenever you try something new in life or when you pursue the major goals in your life. Whenever you feel that something is threatening your basic survival needs such as money, shelter, or food, you can unblock or heal your blocked root chakra. This chakra will respond even when you just have the fear that your basic survival is undermined. There are certain behaviors and emotional issues linked to a blocked Root Chakra. When the Root Chakra is blocked, a person feels anxious, panicked, and threatened. This anxiety can infiltrate our thoughts, which leads to feelings of uncertainty. When this chakra is blocked, a person might not be able to focus or concentrate well. He will lose his concentration over everything.

The sacral chakra is the creative physical center. This chakra controls the urinary tract, pelvic organs, the hips, the bladder, feet, and legs. It also energizes the sexual organs.

The sacral or sexual chakra is polarized negatively, and it is feminine in gender. The color associated with this chakra is orange. If the second chakra is open and clear, you experience feelings of very deep feelings of childlike wonder. The world looks more like a magical place when this chakra is open. However, after puberty, a person experiences blockages in the sacral chakra because of the restrictions and taboos of the society related to sexuality. Because of this blockage, all the wonder and innocence are lost after puberty. This chakra is the focus of your most fundamental and earliest emotions, such as your basic sense of acceptance or rejection, the sense of being alone in this world or belonging to a particular family or group, and the difficulty or ease of an individual may have in connecting with

God. A person's sacral or sexual chakra may be blocked or misaligned when he is stressed or worried about any of the aspects of his sexuality. This chakra will also be blocked if a person is not satisfied in his relationship or is simply trying to experience pleasure in his life. The sacral chakra may also be blocked if you receive any sort of negative feedback, which makes your doubt your capabilities.

The solar plexus chakra is located around your stomach area at the top of the abdomen. The color associated with this chakra is yellow, and the element linked to it is fire. If there is a blockage in this chakra, you will experience many emotional issues and behaviors. You will lose your confidence, and it will be very shaky. However, if the blockage is small, there will be insecurity in any specific area. A larger blockage will cause many self-esteem problems. A person may be haunted by thoughts that he is not good enough. Also, he might feel that he is not able to draw useful challenges from the challenges in his life. Certain physical difficulties are associated with a blocked solar plexus chakra, such as trouble with memory, digestive discomfort, etc.

The heart chakra also acts as a bridge between your mind, body, and soul. When everything is well with this chakra, or it is balanced, a person will be able to be emotionally open. He will also be able to be empathetic towards others and will be able to enjoy a very deep sense of his inner peace. Also, he will be able to understand his emotions on a cognitive level and will feel them fully. Any negative thing related to love will disturb this chakra, such as a grief process, a breakup, any casual cruelty, and a difficult friendship. A blocked heart chakra will result in many emotional issues and behaviors. When this chakra is misaligned or blocked, a person will struggle a lot to relate to other people. He may be impatient in different situations and will be less compassionate. He will not show any empathy to other people. People whose heart chakra is blocked are usually not at peace with themselves, and they find it extremely hard to trust other people.

The throat chakra influences how authentically a person coveys his deepest self to the outer world. An individual's emotional honesty, ownership of needs, directness, etc. are linked to the throat chakra. The color associated with this chakra is blue, and the element linked to it is ether. When a person's throat chakra is balanced, he will be able to speak to others properly and will be well understood by the people around them. Also, he will be able to speak the truth appropriately. A person with an open and balanced throat chakra will be forthright and will not be blunt. There can be a disturbance in your throat chakra if you encounter difficult experiences with communication, such as a bad argument or a tough job interview. The blockage in your throat chakra will lead to certain emotional issues and behaviors. The first major issue is that a person whose fifth chakra is blocked will not be able to say what he really wants to say. A person might feel as if he is stuck holding onto secrets.

The third eye chakra determines a person's ability to see the bigger picture of his life. Also, it determines our intuition and our alignment with this universe. When it is open, a person will be able to adept at picking up signs. Moreover, he will be able to trust his gut feelings and will plan according to his greatest goals in life. Manifestation experiences and the law of attraction successes also relate to the openness of a person's third eye chakra. The third chakra can be misaligned or blocked if someone makes you doubt your own wider purpose. There are many problems associated with a blocked or misaligned chakra. The first major issue is that when a person's third eye chakra is blocked, he might feel that there is no point in what he is doing. He may feel that whatever he does is insignificant. Also, he may be struck by his inability to make decisions in life.

The seventh chakra is the highest chakra, and it determines our spiritual connectivity. This chakra is vital to attain a feeling of peace as well as to establish a life you love. When everything is well with this chakra, or it is balanced, a person will be able to experience feelings of love and joy. He'll be in tune with the beauty in the world around him. To such a person, life will feel glorious, rich, and worthwhile. Remember that any traumatic experience in life may move this chakra out of positive, which causes a person to doubt himself and his purpose. There are certain emotional issues and behaviors which are associated with the blocked or misaligned crown chakra. The first major issue is that when this chakra is disturbed or blocked, a person will not be able to see or observe the beauty of this world. He may experience various symptoms of anxiety or depression and will feel spirituality adrift. Also, he may experience a decline in his overall motivation or excitement.

There are several ways through which you can clean and heal the chakras in your body. The first and most important way is 'meditation.' For each chakra, there are specific meditation techniques that you need to practice. Another major way to heal the chakras is 'affirmations.' Affirmations are statements that possibly replace negative beliefs with positive ones. By saying these phrases or statements to yourself, you will be able to clean and heal your chakras. Another common technique that can be used for healing and cleaning the chakras is 'massages.' By massaging properly, you will be able to heal your chakras easily. Remember one thing that on each chakra, you need to apply different massage methods. You can change your physical states, moods, and emotions by exposing yourself to different types of colors, having different vibrations. By exposing your body to different colors at your home, in your food, and the clothes you wear, you can easily heal the chakras in your body. There is another important way to absorb colors that are wearing color glasses. These glasses absorb the vibrations that are needed in your body. Another important way to clean and heal your chakras is the "chakra stones," which are referred to as healing crystals. The chakra stones contain specific vibrations and colors.

Each chakra in your body has a specified color associated with it. This color is used in the process of Chakra healing. Mostly, a stone with a specified color is used to heal one particular chakra. However, some stones can be used for healing multiple chakras. One example of such stones is Clear quartz.

Yoga is also an important way through which you can clean or heal your chakra.

When the chakras are stuck or blocked, it is better to release the prana or energy using movement. One of the most beneficial and recognized techniques to release stagnant or stuck energy out of your body is 'yoga postures.' Different yoga postures will enable you to be fresh and vital energy back into your body. Another important way for cleaning and healing the chakras in your body is 'music.' Each chakra in your body responds to various sound healing frequencies. One of the most popular techniques is Solfeggio, where different healing sounds are produced using music frequencies. Essential oils are also very important in the process of chakra healing. Generally, these oils are used in combination with different massage techniques.

Copyright © 2020 – Emily C. Heaven

All Rights Reserved